ACTING
FOR FILMS AND TV

ACTING
FOR FILMS AND TV

by Leslie Abbott

PUBLISHING COMPANY

PUBLISHING COMPANY
Belmont, CA 94002

Publisher and Managing Editor: Stuart A. Hoffman
Typography: BookPrep
Cover: Electric Art Studios

Copyright © 1994 by Star Publishing Company

Printed in the United States of America

ISBN: 0-89863-165-3   0987654321

The paper used in this publication meets the requirements
of the American National Standard for Permanence of Paper
for Printed Library Materials Z39.48-1984.

CONTENTS

ACKNOWLEDGEMENTS

No one can write a textbook without considerable help from others: those who precede the author in writing on their subject and those who generously contribute their knowledge and experiences to the author. Among those are:

Woody Allen	Charles Haid
John Allred	Gerard Hurley
Paul Babb	Andrew Johnson
Adrienne Barbeau	Arthur Laurents
Jeffrey Bloom	Ken Letner
Andrew Brye	Charles Martinet
Stan Byrne	Debra Nethery
Yvonne Campbell	Marvin Paige
Francis Ford Coppola	Jim Siebert
Catherine Craig	Joan Simmons
James DePaiva	T. J. Walsh
Nancy Eichler	Mark Williams
William Goldman	Ken White
Michelle Guillermin	Saul Zaentz

To these, and all the writers who have documented information before me, I am deeply indebted and most grateful.

INTRODUCTION

Fascinating business, the entertainment industry. Most especially movies and television. What teenager hasn't dreamed of being part of it either as a rock star or a film-TV actor? Most of us put away such dreams and settle for a more mundane career. This book is addressed to those who hold on to the dream that they may make a career in films and television. Everyone can remember some incident in their life that triggered this ambition. Here is one such occurrence told in the first few pages of a screenplay:

EXT. LONDON, MID-AFTERNOON. VERY DARK.

This is the fog-shrouded London of 1943, a fitting setting for Sherlock Holmes and his trusty aide, Watson, and certainly a confirmation of George and Ira Gershwin's *A Foggy Day in London Town.* (After this kind of pea-soup London fog killed nearly two hundred people in the fifties, the authorities put a stop to the pollution and London's famed fog vanished.)

Groping his way along the street and peering desperately ahead searching for a crosswalk is a MIDDLE-AGED BUSINESSMAN, his umbrella clutched in his right hand to ward off the demons. He steps off the curb to cross the street. We hear the slamming of brakes and an ancient hulk of a taxi grinds to a halt, yellow lights showing feebly through the fog at the man. The gruff voice of the OLD DRIVER can be heard as he leans out of the window.

OLD DRIVER

Get a move on, Gov'ner. We 'aven't all day.

The businessman steps gingerly across the street and the cab once again creeps through the fog.

CUT TO:

INT. LONDON CAB, MID-AFTERNOON. DARK.

The camera slides past the OLD DRIVER to see three young people in the back seat of the cab. They are Americans, their army uniforms pulled tightly around them to ward off the London damp. Sitting in the middle is COSIE, a good-looking, energetic twenty-three year old corporal with an ebullient style. To his right is MARYJEAN, a warm-hearted blondish woman of twenty-four dressed in the uniform of an army nurse. To Cosie's left we see LES, a more subdued GI, no match for the handsome corporal but perhaps a more thoughtful, albeit in-genuous, soldier of nineteen.

COSIE

What time is it?
    Les looks at his watch.

LES

Three o'clock.

MARYJEAN

(peering out window)

PM or AM?

COSIE

God! We'll never make it.

MARYJEAN

Make what?

COSIE

You'll see.

LES

In this atmosphere it's gotta be an opium den.

CUT TO:

EXT. LONDON, MID-AFTERNOON. VERY DARK.

The ancient taxi comes to a halt outside a soot-layered brick building. We first see MARYJEAN climb out of the cab, then COSIE, who moves to the driver to pay the fare, and then LES, who we now see carries a cane; Maryjean reaches over and helps him climb out of the cab. Les walks with a decided limp, but though he's not a cripple, he has obviously lost some of his mobility.

COSIE

This better be it . . . I'd hate to try to find another cab in this fog.

MARYJEAN

Be what, Cosie?

COSIE

You'll find out.

Cosie moves across the sidewalk to a big heavy door. Pulling it open he gestures to his friends to follow him. They start into the blackened building.

CUT TO:

INT. SMALL ROOM, DIMLY-LIT.

Inside the room we see an OLD MAN. In peacetime he'd be retired, but in wartime London every man is needed. COSIE steps up to the man seated behind a desk and hands him a scrap of paper. In the background we see MARYJEAN and LES standing, mystified. The Old Man looks up at a pulsating red light bulb just above the door.

OLD MAN

You'll have to wait a minute . . . they'll be finished in a second . . .

Cosie joins Maryjean and Les in the corner, and after a moment the pulsating red light goes off.

You can go in now . . .

Cosie, with Maryjean and Les right behind him, pulls open the door.

CUT TO:

INT.-EXT. BRIGHTLY-LIT FOREST GLADE. DAY.

Two athletic men, looking very much like Stewart Granger and Dennis Price, are dueling furiously; first one seems to have the advantage, then the other. They are garbed in tights and doublets worn by late eighteenth-century aristocrats. It's as though we were suddenly plunged into the world of THE SCARLET PIMPERNEL.

After a few moments, the more handsome of the two seems to get the better of the other one; the less attractive man falters and falls to the ground as the handsome man towers above him, his saber pointed at the chest of the fallen man. From somewhere we hear the shout, "CUT!" The camera pulls back to reveal that the realistic forest glade is part of a film set that fills much of the soundstage. We see SCHROEDER, the director, CAMILLE, the script girl, the cameraman, and other technicians huddled around the set; at some places on the set we see the logo of the company, "Gainsborough Studios."

In the foreground we see the backs of our THREE YOUNG AMERICANS, bewitched by what they have just witnessed.

And that's how I was introduced to the fascinating world of film making and had my first opportunity to watch actors at work before the camera. Before this episode in my young life, I had planned to be a journalist, but beginning with that Foggy Day in London Town, my interests turned to the movie business.

FILM OR STAGE?

To prepare myself for acting and films, I attended several universities where I majored in drama. I quickly learned that college drama students in those days automatically assumed that theatre represented the pinnacle of the performing arts, and that working in the movies was something you did solely for financial gain. Nowadays that view has changed drastically.

Films at their best are seen as more intellectual, more challenging, and more esthetically satisfying than nearly anything you are likely to experience in the theatre. The most innovative work, the most provocative ideas, more frequently are seen and heard on the screen rather than on the stage.

Sometimes actors have mistakenly assumed that film acting is a lesser art than stage acting; they have been told that performances on camera are simply diminished, smaller versions of what you would do onstage. This perception of what constitutes good film acting is simply untrue, and this book hopes to change that perception.

There are some rewards that an actor can get onstage that are not afforded to the film-TV actor. The theatre provides the opportunity for a satisfying rehearsal period, during which the actor can shape and perfect his characterization; there is time to change a characterization when one has made some wrong choices. No such luck on camera.

The stage actor may have the thrill of having the live audience respond to his artistry; if he plays out of town before a Broadway opening (or in regional theatre at previews), he can gauge his performance in part based on the response of the audience. No such luck on camera.

Working onstage, then, can be enormously gratifying but, with few exceptions, it does not provide a comfortable living. On the other hand, screen acting can be extremely frustrating.

THE DIFFICULTIES

The economics of filmmaking afford little time for rehearsals, scenes are shot out of sequence and in bits and pieces so that it is difficult to create the "through line of action" so important to a well-developed characterization. For actors trained in the theatre, the most extra-ordinary difference in film acting is that you not only have got to know your lines on day one, you will also have to have directed yourself to play them in a certain way. You must have a completely designed characterization ready the first time you come on the set, and all of this must be done without necessarily having discussed the role with the director, without having met the other actors in the scene, and without having rehearsed on the set.

Furthermore, within an hour of this abrupt introduction to film, your first scene has been irretrievably recorded for all time. There's no going back and correcting wrong choices. In addition, the camera records ruthlessly any fraudulent feeling, any lack of emotional commitment to the moment. In terms of being believable on camera, you cannot for a moment have a glint of doubt in your eye. Does that help to explain why so much acting on television seems poor?

Finally, because rehearsals are brief at best, all casting on camera is as much as possible the matching of the actor's persona with the character that he is playing. If they need a five foot three, blond, blue-eyed actor who weighs one hundred and twenty pounds, the casting director will find that exact person somewhere in his files. The film-television actor, with few exceptions, will not play a large range of types; he will be cast for the kind of person he most readily suggests.

A fair part of convincing the casting director that you are right for the role is established in the initial interview before you have actually auditioned for the role. This fact is a good argument for really knowing who you are as a person, truly being in touch with your real feelings, and having the courage to allow yourself to be seen honestly, devoid of all the camouflage and character armor that protect so many of us.

THE REWARDS

But motion picture and television acting also has its special com-pensations. Here the actor can delve more deeply into the psyche of the character and can communicate not only what the character is feeling but what the character is thinking. The actor may incorporate a personalization in a film performance that the limitations of the stage will not allow. The actor's silent moments onscreen may be, as they are in life itself, the most significant, profoundly changing moments of a person's life. Sometimes the camera can record the very thoughts and the discoveries that a character is experiencing; with a fine actor the lens seems to be able to penetrate to the very soul of a human being.

PREPARATION

If you want to act in films and television, then you must go to the movies often. You need to bring the discerning, more sophisticated eye of a professional to your evaluation of why a movie or television show is good or bad. Actors can't be selective, seeing only what's good. You have to see bad movies along with the critically praised ones because you can learn quite a bit from bad movies, particularly once you know why they're bad. You need to watch a movie critically so that as an actor you learn how a fine actor can survive artistically in a poor film, and how an inept actor can weaken a well-written and directed picture.

Before you take a course in acting on camera, you'd better know quite a bit about acting. Time constraints make it impossible for the director-teacher to deal with the basic acting skills an actor must already have acquired in order to do productive work on camera. The actors should already know the tenets of the Stanislavsky system; they should know what is meant by such acting terms as "spine," "objective," "subtext," "preliminary action," "through line of action," "personalization," and "taking the moment." They will probably never hear these terms discussed or mentioned on the set of a film or TV show, but they are necessary parts of the knowledge good actors must have if they are to work effectively on camera. Indeed, most film-TV directors do not know what these terms mean, but the actor must know if he hopes to do good work.

WHAT THIS BOOK DOES

There are two chapters in *Acting for Films and TV* that ordinarily do not appear in a textbook. They deal with the business side of the profession, and I shouldn't think that you will find such information in textbooks having to do with medicine, science, law, education, or any other profession. Why, then, do I include them in this text? In a lifetime as an engineer, lawyer, doctor, educator, or nearly any other profession, you probably would not work with more than five firms or institutions. In the acting profession, whether it be in theatre or films-TV, it is not unusual for a professional to work in hundreds of jobs over the life span of a career.

Seeking and finding work in the acting profession is a very real part of the job and helps to explain why actors are paid so generously when they are actually performing. Many acting students have only a vague sense of this aspect of the profession, and nothing in their training prepares them for the reality of working as an actor. "The Business of the Business" and "Merchandising Your Talent" seek to address this shortcoming and to make it easier for students to launch a viable career once they have left the world of academia.

Although it has long been needed, the economics of filmmaking has caused acting on camera to not be included in the curriculum. Now, with access to reasonably inexpensive video equipment that can emulate in part the film-making process, acting on camera classes will be offered frequently by drama departments. *Acting for Films and TV,* then, is a primer that attempts to cover many aspects of the whole process of acting in the film-TV industry; it is an overview of nearly all aspects of the business from art to commerce.

Acting for Films and TV tries to give enough information about all the aspects of this profession to help the otherwise promising student actor choose whether or not to continue pursuing a career. Each actor must assess his own tenacity, perseverance, and resilience; perhaps the strenuous demands of an acting career are not worth the effort. However, if all that is learned from *Acting for Films and TV* has not dampened the actor's ambition, then it is recommended that the student read more detailed information in such books as Michael Shurtleff's *Audition,* Tony Barr's *Acting on Camera,* Robert Cohen's *Acting Professionally,* and M. K. Lewis' *Your Film-Acting Career.* These books go into greater detail about specific areas of information that an actor must eventually have to become a successful working professional.

While *Acting for Films and TV* covers these elements of the business in abbreviated form, it also addresses some less tangible aspects of working on camera that the reader is not likely to find elsewhere. Specifically, the information regarding "Attributes of A Good Film Actor," "Stardom," and "The Actor and the Director" are unique to this book. Near the end of the book are a series of scenes, mostly from original screenplays, that can be used in acting on camera classes. With the exception of Woody Allen's scene from **Manhattan,** none of these screenplays have been made into theatrical films, so the actor does not have another actor's example to use as a guideline in creating the role. With few exceptions, these are scenes that can be shot on college campus locales.

Acting for Films and TV offers easy-to-follow guidelines to almost all the experiences that an actor encounters in films and television. Now, let's take that step into the complicated world of the film-TV actor . . . set the slate, and roll'em for Scene 1, Take 1.

CHAPTER 1

NUTS AND BOLTS: THE BASICS FOR ACTING ON CAMERA

The first time that I appeared on camera was a nightmare. At that time I had done at least sixty plays onstage, but none of them had prepared me for the sheer terror I experienced when that great huge 35-millimeter camera loomed in on me and the leading man. You feel as though the well-being of the whole world depends on you, and you experience camera fright equal to the stage fright that was your lot the first time you stepped onstage.

This fear, of course, is unreasonable, but the making of films is so different in atmosphere from theatre that it is no surprise that anxiety can strike at the heart of even the most experienced actor when he makes his first appearance on camera. You are invariably surrounded by hordes of people who seem stunningly indifferent to your performance. They are preoccupied with so many other activities essential to the making of the film that your acting performance seems simultaneously of no importance and of the greatest importance. As producer-director Charles Haid, probably best known for his memorable portrayal of Renko in *Hill Street Blues,* describes it, "You've got to know what the guy standing over there on the set does. In your most private acting moments there will be a guy chewing gum and talking to someone about his golf game. They are no respecter of art in some ways . . . but on every set you go on, when they say 'roll please' or 'camera,' then 'speed,

On location APOCALYPSE NOW

The first time you appear in a movie can be an overwhelming experience. How would you like to face this formidable crew from *APOCALYPSE NOW*, a film burdened with nearly every disaster known to man. Perched high on his director's chair in the background is Francis Ford Coppola. In your wildest imagination you could never foresee the amount of people and resources that need to be assembled just to shoot the simplest of scenes. Around you are gathered various artisans — grips, gaffers, best boys, costumers, make-up artists, along with the director, cinematographer, script supervisor — and they all depend on your acting contribution once the word "Action!" is called out. Now everything depends on you, the actor. Suddenly the 35 millimeter camera seems so large and ominous, the task nearly overwhelming. What if you blow a line? What if you miss your mark by a couple of inches? What if your interpretation doesn't satisfy the director? Everything then grinds to a halt, all that raw stock running through the camera is wasted, all of those people running around the set on various tasks are being kept waiting while you flounder. You suddenly become aware that your mistake is costing an enormous amount of money. It's at such a time that it takes courage, a strong ego, and incredible strength of character to somehow plow through all the pressure and triumph.

sound, action,' that's when everybody stops talking; the concentration for that moment is on what is happening in the action of the scene . . . that's what all the preparation has been for . . . and the actors who are good can really shut the whole world out and turn the heat up."

The first day on the set is always a lesson under fire, but it does help if you've prepared yourself by knowing that in the course of this first day these events will probably transpire.

ACTION. The most riveting word for actors is "action!" This word has two meanings for the actor, both of which are important. "Action!" is the word that the director uses when he wants the actors to start performing. Usually this crucial word is preceded by the following phrases, all of which have particular meaning.

QUIET ON THE SET! The process begins when the assistant director calls out "quiet on the set!" On a soundstage this may be accompanied by the shrill clanging of a bell and the flashing of red warning lights outside the soundstage entrance.

CAMERA (or ROLL, PLEASE, TURN OVER). After quiet on the set is finally achieved, you will hear the director say "camera" (or sometimes "roll, please, turn over"), which is the signal for the cameraman to begin rolling the film. Once the film is rolling through the camera at the proper speed (and this takes a few moments) the cameraman will call out,

SPEED. This tells the director that the camera is ready to shoot the scene.

SOUND. After the cameraman calls out "speed," the sound man informs the director that the sound is being recorded properly by calling out "sound."

MARK IT. As soon as the cameraman (focus puller) hears "sound," he then says "mark it," which signals the slateboard person who holds the slate in front of the camera lens to call out the title of the film or TV film, the scene number, and which take this may be. This careful documentation then can be read by the editor on the film when he is cutting the movie or TV show and also can be heard spoken by the slateboard person. Such meticulous documentation assists the editor in piecing together all the film shot preparatory to putting together a rough cut. Using the script supervisor's notes coupled with the identification of each piece of film by the slateboard person makes the editor's job easier.

ACTION! Once the slateboard person has spoken the information regarding the scene and the take, the director calls out "action!" Sometimes the director will not say "action!" immediately; it may be for technical reasons, such as making sure that the slateboard person's shadow is not hitting the back scenery. Perhaps the cameraman may point out that the microphone boom is showing in the frame. All these technical mishaps, which frequently stall the shooting of a scene, are frustrating to the actor who has prepared himself psychologically for the scene and then finds the scene aborted while yet another technical adjustment is made. However, once the actors have heard the magic word "action!" they should begin.

CUT! When the actor hears the director call "cut!" at the conclusion of a scene, it is wise to keep acting for five to ten seconds more, staying inside the character and continuing to experience whatever the character is experiencing at that moment. Occasionally the extra moments played silently and in response to either the internal experience or as a reaction to the preceding action of the character may be useable by the editor since the sound of the director's "cut" can be deleted from the soundtrack. The actor should never make the mistake of dropping out of character the moment the dialog or the physical action of the scene is completed; sometimes the assimilation of what the character has been experiencing that we see on the actor's face or in his body language after the dialog and physical action have been completed can be enormously effective on camera. How the actor's character is registering what was just experienced may look wonderful on film, and the producer, director, or editor may decide to incorporate that moment into the final cut.

Certainly, the actor must never stop a take for any reason except injury or death once the director has called "action!" The actor keeps on performing regardless of whatever mishaps or dialog problems may occur; only the director, or the star in some instances, may cause the film take to be stopped before it has been completed. Sometimes an experienced star will stop a take before it's completed because he knows it is not playing well. Since he is the most important person on the set, almost always far more important than the director, he can have that prerogative. No one else other than the director, and occasionally the cameraman, can initiate a cut. Stars or very important principal players will sometimes purposefully "blow" a line or muff a piece of business so that a take will have to be redone. A clever star or principal player will never acknowledge that he has intentionally caused the scene to need to be reshot since this might cause friction with the director. The actor knows that the director, especially in television, is accountable to the production company and that the director is always being urged to complete as many scenes as possible each day.

Economic expediency on the part of the production company and, hence, the director, will often dictate whether a take is satisfactory. The star or principal player may sometimes make a "mistake" simply to protect his reputation. On the other hand, any actor who does not have such clout would be ill-advised to employ the same tactics; such an actor would be jeopardizing the possibility of ever working for that production company again. Given all this stopping and starting in the putting together of this elaborate process called filmmaking, it is not unusual for only three minutes of a movie to be shot in a twelve-hour day.

ACTION! There is a second meaning for the word action that is often relevant to the actor. This is when "action" refers to the physical action that the actors employ in the scene. Usually a director will run through the scene with the actors one or two times to set the physical action. Sometimes this action is determined before the camera moves are set, and sometimes the camera moves are chosen first and then the actors' moves are set. In a master shot both the actors and the camera are likely to move a number of times. These moves are carefully planned and must be consistently adhered to by the actors during the action since their physical distance from the camera lens may change and the focus puller must alter the camera focus to accommodate these differences in distance.

Consequently, it is always important that the actor always end up on his "marks." When you hear actors talking about "hitting their marks,"

*Daniel Day-Lewis and Lena Olin in **THE UNBEARABLE LIGHTNESS OF BEING***
The actor needs to know how the scene is going to be framed; he or she may get an idea from the emotional content of the material, the proximity of the camera, the discussions between cinematographer and cameramen, the crew, perhaps even the director. Sometimes, however, the camera may be positioned some distance from the action but the lens will be focused so that the sequence is tightly framed, allowing the actor relatively little room for movement. You want your gestures and action to stay inside the frame for maximum effectiveness. For that reason, whenever possible the actor should know how the scene is being framed.

they are referring to those marks generally put on the floor with masking tape that indicate the position of their feet at the end of each move that the actor makes in the scene. There are any number of reasons why an actor must get to his marks. Perhaps the cinematographer needs to have the actor be hit by a "key" light at a certain moment in the sequence. It may be that at a given point in the action the use and placement of light and shadow will enhance the dramatic meaning of the moment, and this is dependent on the actor's being exactly at a certain place on the set. It may be something as simple as hitting your mark so that your face is in focus on camera. Another factor to be considered is that if you do not hit your mark, you may destroy the composition of the shot. With good directors and cinematographers, the composition of the scene is not simply to be beautiful to the eye but to evoke the correct psychological response from the audience. Finally, if you do not hit your marks properly you may mask another actor. Woe to the actor who inadvertently masks a star!

FRAME. It is extremely important when a shot is being taken that the actor know what is likely to appear in the frame. The word frame can mean several different things depending on how it is used: (1) It means one single picture on a piece of motion picture film, (2) It means the boundaries of the screen image, and this second descriptive term is frequently important to the actor, since it assists him in knowing what dimensions he can comfortably play in. For example, if the frame is filled with most of his body, then the actor does not wish to gesticulate in such a way that his arms, legs, or head go outside the frame. If his head is filling much of the frame in a closeup and he keeps bobbing back and forth from left to right, the audience will get a kind of seasickness from watching him. (3) It means that the director and the cinematographer are composing the shot so as to include, exclude, or emphasize certain elements. This may be important to the actor in choosing the manner of movement he employs in the sequence.

SHOTS. A "shot" or "take" is essentially the same. As long as what you see is photographed by the camera whose film keeps rolling without stopping, you are looking at one shot. For example, the camera may stay in one place and pan with a boy running down the street, or it can dolly (that is, move on wheels) with the boy as he runs down the street from one corner to the next. If the camera interrupts your view of the boy so that you see him running around the first corner and then you see him from another point of view (POV), panting at the next corner, you will have seen two shots.

TAKE. Although we have just said that a shot and a take are essentially the same, a take may sometimes mean something slightly different. If a director doesn't like the way a scene plays in front of the camera, he may shoot the scene over again. Each shot, even though it is a repetition of the same scene taken from the same camera position, is called a take. Eventually, when the director has satisfied himself that he has a good take that he'll want to use in the final movie, he will say "that's a take!" This signals the company that they can move on to the next setup. At this point, it should be mentioned that actors who do not require many takes since they are well prepared and have excellent concentration are highly respected, because they save time and money for the production company.

The actor will usually hear the director telling either the "talent" (the performers) or camera crew what kind of shot is wanted for a given sequence, and this is important for the actor to know whenever possible since it makes it possible for him to make the right choices of physical action within the shot. For these reasons, whenever possible, it is important to know what the shot will physically encompass in the frame. Often the director is so busy that asking him would be ill advised; a quiet word with the cameraman will probably elicit the information you need.

ESTABLISHING SHOT. This refers to a shot showing the location of the action and/or the arrangement and physical juxtaposition of the characters appearing in the action. For example, in a scene in which a number of people are involved in the action, the director should establish at the beginning of the scene an approximation of the characters' physical distance and relationship to each other for the audience. Once the audience knows the physical relationships of the various characters, then the director can go on to show these characters in various combinations, including medium shots, two shots, and closeups.

MASTER SHOT. A wide shot that includes one or more actors. It follows the movement of the characters in the scene. A master shot may be uninterrupted from the beginning of a scene to the end of a scene, or it may be interrupted several times because the director knows that he will break it up into an edited form that includes portions of the master shot, over-the-shoulder shots, and closeups. The master shot is important since it covers all the material essential to the coherent storytelling of this particular scene in the script. If there should be any parts of the scene that have inadvertently not been covered by any other kinds of shots, the editor then always has the recourse of returning to the master shot to keep the storytelling understandable to the audience.

Once the director has completed a master shot that covers all the pertinent action of the scene, he then may call for a number of other kinds of shots, which will be edited together in the final cut:

OVER-THE-SHOULDER shots are those in which we look across the back of one actor to the face of another. Over-the-shoulder shots are usually done in pairs so that the editor can match these shots as the director cuts back and forth from one character to the other.

CLOSEUP shots are those in which a face or a small detail fills the frame, taken either by setting the camera close to the subject or by using a long-focus-length lens. In relationship to an actor, a closeup usually refers to a shot of the face alone although, of course, there may be a closeup of hands or feet, or of any part of the body. Whatever shot is chosen to put in the frame is based on the psychological and esthetic sense of the scene that the director wishes to communicate at a given moment. A gifted director will have excellent intuitive skills and usually know exactly what kind of shot to put into the frame. Unfortunately, there are lots of less-gifted directors who make poor choices with a consequent diminishing of effectiveness. This kind of choice making is beyond the control of the actor and, once again, substantiates what a collaborative art form filmmaking is and how difficult it is for the actor to control the effectiveness of his performance.

Sometimes a sequence may be shot partially or totally in closeup without the actor's being aware of it. During a take, the camera may not dolly in closer to you but nonetheless is zooming in for a tighter shot. If you are central to the scene that is being shot, you should ask beforehand what kind of shot is being set up. Knowing what is encompassed in the shot and how you will be framed will assist you in knowing how to gauge the scale of your performance. If the shot tightens during the sequence to a closeup of you, the director (or cameraman) will tell you how much room you have to move; if they don't, ask! If you are told that you have two inches to move to the left with your head and two inches to move to your right with your head, then that is exactly how much room you have to move without your head partly leaving the frame. Generally speaking, you can play with broader movement in the master shot (or long shot), with somewhat smaller movement in the medium shot, and almost exclusively with your face in the closeups. It's in the closeups that your listening and thinking in character will most clearly be shown; let us hope that you are really listening and thinking!

Certain actors use their hands effectively in closeups; they will hold their heads, brush a hand through their hair, or touch their mouths with a hand. Remember that nearly half the world's population have oral character formations and constantly have their hands near their mouths. Observe people while they are unaware and you will learn that this is true. If it is so in real life, why don't more actors do it on film? It gives a performance more credibility, makes an actor interesting on camera, and is often more truthful.

When you are the on-camera actor in a closeup, never shift your focus from one eye to the other. Why? Because it's natural when you look at something that one of your eyes leads. If you are in a closeup and you change whichever eye you're leading with, it will be noticeable on the screen. It's most disconcerting to an audience. In a closeup, the eyes tell more than any other part of your face. Be careful not to make faces; it telegraphs to the audience what they are supposed to feel and they unconsciously resent your using such a tactic. They don't want to be told what they should feel; they want to arrive at their emotional responses unconsciously, spontaneously. Just rely on your character's thought processes and your face will make the right choices without your "indicating" a phony emotion.

Some time ago I read a teacher's suggestion that actors "act" in front of the mirror as a means of preparing for their closeups on camera. It's an appalling idea. First, it's no good practicing in front of the mirror because in the mirror is you, not the person you are playing in the movie. Second, you cannot be in character and simultaneously observe and evaluate your character's physical manifestations.

While one actor is being shot in closeups from the point of view of the other actor, the off-camera actor stands alongside the camera and plays his portion of the scene from there. A conscientious, intelligent actor will play with as much emotional commitment off camera as he does when the director is shooting his on-camera closeups; he does this because he wants his acting partner to be as good as possible since each person's performance complements the other. He also does it so that his acting partner will return the favor when his closeups are being shot. If he is fortunate enough to be the actor whose closeups are shot second, he can use his off-camera work with the other actor to refine and enhance his performance. Unfortunately, some actors will save their energy when they are off camera feeding dialog to the on-camera actor. When this happens, the on-camera actor should somehow play to what the off-camera actors should be doing rather than what they are actually doing.

Occasionally stars will not feel it is necessary for them to spend their time working when they are not on camera. At such times the dialog may be read by the script supervisor or someone else. Such stars, regardless of their elevated status in Hollywood, are rude and inconsiderate. Most likely they achieved their positions because they had a certain look appropriate for some roles and their talents may be quite small. Regardless of their current star status, this lack of professionalism usually results in a short-lived career.

In shooting closeups, the actors need to remember that the editor will be cutting the film so that it moves back and forth between the two actors. The editor needs a bit of space on the film to cut from one actor's dialog to the other actor's dialog. Therefore, while shooting closeups the screen actor does not pick up cues as tightly as an actor would do playing the same scene onstage. Both the on-camera and the off-camera actors while shooting closeups take a beat following the other actor's dialog before responding with their own dialog. Although the beat may be three to four seconds long before you begin the dialog, you have no way of knowing exactly at what point the editor will cut to you on the finished print. Consequently, it is very important that although you have not yet responded vocally to the other actor's cue, you fill those silent moments of three to four seconds before you speak with the strong inner life of your character. If the inner life of your character is supported by the right kind of internal energy, your character will hold the interest of the audience even if the editor has cut to you several seconds before you speak.

There are limits to how much you can move in a closeup, but you can figure that there is probably at least four inches of space on both sides of your face within which you can move. When the camera is that close to your face, it offers you a superb opportunity to give a more subtle and heartfelt performance. If the inner life of your character is strongly experienced and if your energy is appropriate to the meaning of the moment, the camera will love you whether you are speaking or silent.

Naturally, actors want to get as many closeups as they can. By so doing they are establishing their presence within the film and becoming more identifiable to the movie-going audience as an individual personality. Becoming more identifiable as an individual can lead the actor to obtaining larger roles as he develops recognition from the audience.

In closeups or over-the-shoulder shots, the actor must avoid playing directly into the lens. Always play slightly to the left or the right of the lens when you're in a closeup talking to another character. This should happen automatically if your acting partner is standing alongside the camera and you talk directly into his eyes. When shooting your close-ups, look at your acting partner's eye that is nearest to the camera; this action builds a greater intimacy with the audience. As audiences, we have sometimes seen actors talk directly into the camera lens and it is disconcerting; it forces the viewer in the movie theater or in front of the television set into a direct confrontation with the actor and destroys the illusion that the viewer is watching a natural situation as an unseen observer.

MEDIUM CLOSE shots are those taken with the camera at a slight distance from the actor. These shots probably include the face, neck, and shoulders of the actor. Closeups and medium-close shots are usually employed when two actors are engaged in a significant conversation or interaction with each other. These shots cut back and forth from one character to the other in the final edited version. Knowledgeable actors know that their silent reactions to their acting partners may be their most effective moments on screen. They give as much energy and involvment to their silent responses to the other character(s) as they do to their verbal exchanges. This is why intelligent actors always create a strong subtext whenever they are on camera. An actor's thoughts can register potently on camera, and an audience will feel privy to what is going on in the mind of the character the actor is playing.

MEDIUM shots are taken with the camera at a mid-range point from the actor(s). Frequently such a shot may include two people in the frame and is sometimes referred to as a "two shot." This medium shot usually reveals the people in it from their knees or waist up.

MEDIUM LONG shots are taken at a distance from the subject, but closer than a long shot. Subtleties in action and facial expression will be lost in such a shot, but an actor can help judge his movement when he realizes that this is a medium long shot. When the director calls for a two shot he may mean a medium shot, as discussed previously, that includes two people in the shot, but sometimes the two shot will be focused tighter and the two heads of the actors in the shot will fill the frame. One condition that surprises actors new to the camera is how close the two actors appearing in a scene together may be positioned to each other. It seems as though you are practically on top of each other and so close that an uncomfortable intimacy is suggested. Space registers differently on camera, however, and while the actors may feel that they are much too physically close to each other, on camera the actors will seem appropriate and just right. This is a circumstance in which the actor must trust the director's judgment and not make an issue of the positioning.

Another factor that is important to the actor in terms of his choice making is the camera angle of the shot. This term means the angle of the view of the actors that is established by the position of the camera. For example, a high-angled shot means that the camera is above the actors looking down on them. At such a time, it is important to remember that tilting your head down to convey sorrow or introspection or profound concern, whatever emotion that leads to a natural lowering of the head, may not be effective on camera. Since actors usually begin their careers in the theatre, it is natural for them to lower their heads at such moments. This action on camera may simply result in the audience's seeing only the top of your head and not having any clear-cut idea of what your character is experiencing emotionally. Where intuitively you would lower your head, during a high-angle shot you may need to do just the opposite. You may lift your head upward and away from the other character(s) in the scene to suggest what your character is experiencing emotionally.

A low-angled shot means that the camera is looking up at the subject. This frequently is done to communicate to the audience that the character is menacing or very powerful in relationship to the other characters. It is usually an unflattering shot for the actor involved, but when used appropriately, it can be most effective. In this kind of shot tilting your head down towards the camera can suggest that you may wish to inflict pain or that you are threatening. No directors have used low-angle shots more effectively than Orson Welles did in *Touch of Evil* and John Huston did in *The Maltese Falcon.*

DOLLY SHOT. Often an actor will be involved in a dolly shot that may or may not include dialog. Dolly shots either involve the camera moving towards or away from the actor(s). Sometimes the camera dollies at a continually equal distance from the actors as they are walking or running. In such a shot, the actor is moving towards the camera while the camera in motion is usually moving backwards while maintaining the same distance from the subject during the entire shot. If the actor is involved in the dolly shot with other performers, it is important that everyone maintain the same proportionate distance from each other and from the camera throughout the scene. Unexpected changes in the speed of the actors' walking may result in the actors' either getting too close or becoming too distant from the camera. In either case this erratic changing of distance from the camera causes the film to lose its sense of reality; the audience becomes aware of the camera as an intrusive force, and the film stops telling its story effectively.

In a dolly shot, another factor that must be taken into consideration by the actor is that the microphone picking up the sound may also be moving. The actor needs to consider where that microphone is at all times if he wishes his performance to be clearly heard. All these mechanical factors are frustrating to an actor and sometimes make it doubly difficult to give a truthful, believable performance. Nothing is gained by fretting over or complaining about these elements. The actor who will enjoy success in films is the one who adapts to the limitations imposed by the camera and microphone and still gives a truthful, believable performance. In all the art forms, the limitations of the medium help to shape the esthetics and discipline of the art. The actor who learns to work effectively within the technical confines of the motion picture medium is rewarded by film's greater ability to reveal the inner thoughts of a character while capturing a greater environmental reality.

TRACKING SHOT. Another shot in which the actor may be moving and continually photographed is called a tracking shot. This is a shot taken from a moving object, possibly a motor vehicle with a camera mounted on it, or a camera mounted on a pedestal on wheels that is on a track that runs parallel to the subject, whether that be actors, an army tank, or cowboys racing on their horses down a canyon. The advantage of using a camera on a pedestal with wheels mounted on a track is that you can photograph subjects moving across rough terrain without the camera's movement being jerky. By putting the camera on tracks, you eliminate the bouncing and unsteady movement that calls attention to the camera and thus becomes poor storytelling. The same principle of keeping proportionate distance to other actors and being consistent in the speed of your movement that applies to working in a dolly shot is pertinent to a tracking shot.

LOOPING. Sometimes, in these dolly and tracking shots, it is difficult to record the voices of the actors properly. In fact, in nearly all location shooting there are so many variables involved that sometimes the recording of sound is faulty. Then it becomes necessary in post production to loop the sound in those scenes in which the actors' voices were not recorded effectively. This entails the actors' sitting in a sound studio watching the film and rereading the lines into a microphone and lip synching their speeches to the movement of their lips onscreen. It is not easy and the actor who does it well is highly valued.

There's a pertinent sidebar to this problem of sometimes having to loop an actor's voice in post production. A producer I know was doing a low-budget film that was shot mostly on location in the ranch country near Los Angeles. He had cast for his female lead a young actress whom a great many people felt would probably have an impressive career. During the shoot, the sound man continually complained that she was nearly inaudible and must speak louder. The director joined the sound man in warning her that she could not be heard, but she insisted that speaking louder would harm the truthfulness of her performance, so she continued the same level of vocal projection throughout the shooting. At the preview of the movie, to her horror she watched her mouth open and close to the sounds of another actress who had looped all of her lines for the film during post production. Hollywood is essentially a small town, and the word got around that she had been difficult on the set and had cost the production company more money than they could afford. Since then, she has played only minor roles, and now, as a not-so-young actress, she makes most of her living teaching method acting.

TILT SHOT. When the camera is on an actor who is seated and the actor rises to his feet with the camera lens moving upward with him as he rises, this is a tilt shot. The camera remains in place but rotates vertically on its axis so that the actor is continually reframed. It is important for the actor to rise in a smooth and slower-than normal movement so that the cameraman can follow him; the camera may not be able to tilt up or down quickly enough to keep the actor in the frame if the actor moves too fast. When rising, it is natural for a person to bend his body forward since the momentum of a body leaning forward makes standing up easier. But if he rises this way when the camera is on a pedestal higher than the chair in which the actor is seated, all we will see in the frame is the top of the actor's head. Actors rising from chairs should make sure that their body and head alignments are straight forward and rely exclusively on their legs to lift them to a standing position.

One can see how technical the whole process of making films is. John Huston once said that an actor's life is one of waiting: waiting for the setup to be ready technically, waiting for the lights to be focused, waiting for the myriad adjustments that sometimes are only caught by one of the crew at the moment just before shooting. When the actor has a grasp of the technical aspects of film production and comes to understand why there are so many delays in shooting, then the actor will not be annoyed by the "hurry up and wait" nature of moviemaking. You learn to accommodate your moods to fit this collective effort of so many to create art.

CHAPTER 2

ABOVE THE LINE
BELOW THE LINE

If you are the kind of person who as a kid read all the copy on the sides of cereal boxes, then you are certainly the kind of adult who reads the credits as they roll by at the end of a film. Certainly some of the job titles must have piqued your curiosity, such as "gaffer" and "best boy." Well, if you are going to work as an actor in motion pictures, some of these curious titles become an important part of your knowledge.

In motion picture budgets, the personnel employed and their job descriptions are broken down into two categories: above-the-line people and below-the-line people. Above-the-line people include creative and performing personnel such as the producer, associate producer(s), director, cinematographer, art director, writers, musical director, and actors. The producer is directly in charge of all these related functions and works closely with all the personnel listed.

Below-the-line people include production manager, line producer, assistant director(s), camera operators, script supervisor, grips, gaffers, makeup artists, hairdressers, sound technicians, wardrobe people, set decorators, and myriad other jobs, depending upon the breadth of the production.

This is a kind of job description of those people grouped among the above-the-line personnel:

PRODUCER. In the beginning there was a man or woman with an idea. They read a novel that they thought would make a good movie. Or they saw a script that they became convinced would be the greatest thing since *Gone with the Wind.* For whatever reason, making this property into a movie became this person's obsession. This person then is responsible for putting together everything it takes to make a movie, from the artistic elements to the money. Theirs is a much-maligned job with joking images of crass cigar-smoking moguls conjured up in our minds. Their work often includes conceiving the production, finding the appropriate writers, shepherding the script along until it's camera ready, finding and negotiating contracts with the appropriate stars and supporting players, and finding and choosing the right director likely to be empathetic to the script and capable of marshalling all the various forces to make the film. He or she is likely to follow the production right into postproduction work and be a component in the way the distribution company sells the picture to the public. Producers are notable for their courage, tenacity, energy, and bulldog-like determination. Confusion arises because each time a movie is made, the producer's functions are always a little different. Just keep in mind that without a producer, the movie would never get made.

EXECUTIVE PRODUCER. This person gets top credit and sometimes, as with Saul Zaentz who has produced *One Flew Over the Cuckoo's Nest, Amadeus* and *The Unbearable Lightness of Being,* deserves it. More often, he's either the person who put up the most money or who got the studio to put up the most money and who will claim credit if the film is a success.

ASSOCIATE PRODUCER. Sometimes this person deserves the credit for the hours of toil he or she has given. More often it's likely that they brought in additional money at a crucial time. Sometimes they are the person who does the myriad daily organization details. Sometimes their title is assistant producer.

DIRECTOR. The most important person on the set, the director tells everyone what to do and sometimes where to go. The director generally will be the one most closely associated with the creative decisions involved in the final look and feel of the production. He or she is likely to contribute ideas to the writers before the final script is approved, communicate with the art director and the cinematographer prior to production on the "look" of the film, and confer with the principal actors in defining their characters and their relevance to the whole film. Once the shoot begins, he becomes the "general" who runs the operation. The director, then, becomes during the course of preproduction, shoot, and postproduction the planner, creative artist, and the executor. He or she must be concerned—usually in conjunction with the producer—with the ordering and reserving of all studio facilities and requirements. The director must lay out the basic scenic design and graphic elements with the art director, usually scout locations with the art director, and work with the cinematographer on the visual aspects of the film. He develops a working script, one that has schematic plans for all the shots and camera transitions, and basic plans for the staging of scenes, a sense of what he will want to put into the frame that we, the audience, will see at each given moment of the film. The director must, as much as possible, foresee that which is likely to happen during the shoot, and before the shoot even commences. He should be quickly able to make adaptations based on all kinds of unforeseen happenings, such as rainy weather; it could mean adjusting from a scene originally planned to be shot at midnight on a dark sports field to one that will be shot in a deserted warehouse. Even if the director is incompetent, this is an overwhelming job, and a fine director is much to be admired. Leadership, taste, judgment, a strong visual eye, an ability to communicate, and a degree in psychology are all helpful skills.

SCREENWRITER. In the beginning there was the word, and screenwriters constantly need to remind ego-driven directors with a predilection for the billing "Film by . . ." that the screenwriter's contribution is a major one. Screenwriters develop the plot and then the dialog. More often than not, a very fine script was written by one person, a good script by two people, and a terrible script by committee. Each time a portion of the script is rewritten during production, the new material is printed on a different-colored mimeograph paper. On occasion I have done a script with five different page colors! These multicolored scripts are more likely to be the norm on a television show where there is never enough time and people are always working against a deadline.

CINEMATOGRAPHER. Sometimes called the director of photography. A key person in making the film, the cinematographer, in collaboration with the director and the art director, determines how the film will look. He supervises all the lighting involved in the shoot and supervises and instructs the camera crew. He is the final arbiter in tandem with the director of what and how everything shot appears in the frame.

ART DIRECTOR. Sometimes known as the production designer, this person, along with the director and cinematographer, is responsible for the overall look of a film. He scouts the locations before the director, eliminates the worst, and shows him the best. He designs interiors when the sequence is being shot on a soundstage. He figures out what the environment should look like for each sequence.

MUSIC DIRECTOR. Either composes the music or assembles the music from various sources that underscores the film and does so much to enhance the desired mood. He frequently conducts the orchestra that records the score for the picture.

Moving to the below-the-line personnel, these are the people with whom an actor sometimes deals:

FIRST ASSISTANT DIRECTOR. The person whose corresponding job in the theatre is called stage manager. The assistant director, who may be the nicest guy in the world, is still the "fall guy" for everyone's complaints. It's his task to make sure everyone shows up on time for the shooting, keeps extras from trying to hog the camera, and gets to say "quiet on the set!"

SECOND ASSISTANT DIRECTOR. Does those things the first assistant director doesn't have time to do. It's one of the truisms of the motion picture business that first and second directors almost never get to be directors. How do you get to be a director? Find the money to finance your first low-budget film. If it makes money at the box office, you're off and running as a director. Or, barring finding the money to finance your first picture, you might after many years move up the ranks from screenwriter, editor, or cinematographer. Are there any other ways? Almost never.

SECOND UNIT DIRECTOR. This is the person who does a few day's shooting out of the country or somewhere on location when the director either doesn't want to go or doesn't have the time to go. Second unit work usually doesn't involve stars, usually has little or no dialog, and rarely contains any significant story-telling elements of the script. It very often includes car chases, explosions, and dangerous action. Most of this work is done with stuntmen, sometimes made up and dressed up to look like the stars. It's foolish to use major stars to do their own stunts since their injury could jeopardize finishing the picture. Forget the "macho" stuff, guys!

SCRIPT SUPERVISOR. This person is invaluable to any film production. He or she stands or sits behind the camera and takes copious notes detailing every aspect of the shooting of each take. This might include noting the clothes an actor is wearing, the hand he uses to pick up a telephone, the recording of the dialog as it was spoken (and varies from the dialog the writer has put in the script), tells the slateboard person what number to put on the slate, and records the number of takes and their length. The script supervisor is responsible for the continuity of a film, making sure that shots match and have been completed as called for in the script. The script supervisor makes sure that costumes, props, and makeup remain consistent in sequential scenes, even though they may have not been shot on the same day or in the same location and rarely in sequence.

SET DECORATOR. Finds the right prop and puts it in the right place on the set. He sometimes chooses fabrics, drapes, and swags, and may upholster furniture to color coordinate with the environment. He dabs color on a wall when it will enhance the set. He fulfills the art director's wishes.

PROPERTY MASTER. He does the same thing a prop man does on a stage production, and is responsible for all the movable, inanimate objects on the set and those carried by actors.

CONSTRUCTION MANAGER. He is in charge of getting what needs to be built built. Once upon a time, in the earlier days of Hollywood when everything was shot on a soundstage or on the lot, nearly everything the camera saw was built by the construction manager's crew.

CONSTRUCTION CREW. They do the work the construction manager needs done.

STORYBOARD ARTIST. Not used by every production, but when used he puts the script into comic book form; this provides a guide for the director in putting together visually how a scene will look. It often is a visualization of the metaphors the director gave the storyboard artist in describing how he wanted a scene to look.

COSTUME DESIGNER. Sometimes this job is just a matter of pulling the right rags off the rack, but more often it requires lots of research for authenticity and myriad drawings that are not only historically correct and psychologically enhancing but will look good on the star. This is not such an easy job when the star is fifty pounds overweight and wearing a corset to cinch in his gut.

COSTUMERS. Sometimes they're just called "wardrobe." Not "wardrobe people," just "wardrobe." They help the actors into and out of their clothes. They mend things, adapt, and improvise. They spend a lot of valuable but necessary time reassuring the actor that they just look great in the chosen clothes.

MAKEUP ARTIST. Works long and carefully to make the beautiful people beautiful. Just puts pancake makeup on the others.

SPECIAL EFFECTS MAKEUP. Creates cuts, bruises, horrific monsters, and packets that spurt blood when the villains or cowboys or soldiers are wounded, machine-gunned, or knifed.

LOCATION MANAGER. Nails down the locations the art director wants to use. He negotiates price, figures out where to put the owners while using their property—preferably on a desert island six thousand miles from their property. He then mollifies people when their property is being mangled by a large, insensitive cast and crew.

CASTING DIRECTOR. He screens those actors who are possible contenders for roles the movie. As potential actors are narrowed down to two or three possibilities for each role, the casting director then works with the producer(s) and director in choosing those who are finally cast. A casting director's continuing in their job depends on their finding the right actors for the roles.

CAMERA OPERATOR. Runs the camera during filming.

FIRST ASSISTANT CAMERA. Sometimes called "focus puller." Adjusts the focus during master shots and traveling shots, and makes sure the camera has film.

SECOND ASSISTANT CAMERA. Also known as "slateboard person" or "clapper boy." He is responsible for keeping the slate with clapper current. He checks frequently with the script supervisor, since they must be recording identical information.

SOUND OPERATOR. Also known as sound mixer. This is a key job with the responsibility for how the film sounds.

BOOM OPERATOR. Handles microphones hanging from extended long poles above performers.

KEY GRIP. Chief stagehand on set. He supervises the crew.

GRIPS. Stagehands in movie-talk terms. They move sets and furniture and whatever else needs to be moved around.

GAFFER. Aha! You thought I'd never get to it. The gaffer is the chief electrician responsible for the lighting on the set. He takes his orders from the cinematographer.

BEST BOY. If he's the gaffer's chief assistant, then he is the "best boy electric"; if he's the key grip's chief assistant, then he is the "best boy grip."

CHAPTER 3

ATTRIBUTES OF
A GOOD FILM ACTOR

"God, I'm good-looking! Isn't it wonderful that people find me so attractive? And look at my body! Lord knows what kind of fantasies it sparks in my fans!" Too many actors start their careers having this attitude and ten years later are sadly watching both their fading profiles and their fading careers.

"Tell me how to be a successful actor? I don't want to be just a flash in the pan. I want acting to be my life!" That's what the reader wants to know and that's why this chapter must deal in part with intangibles. How does one define the attitudes, work methods, and personalities that seem to be shared by most successful actors?

The strength of good film actors is that they're never satisfied and smug about themselves and their work. Actors whose careers have spanned many years of filmmaking, people such as the late Melvyn Douglas, Spencer Tracy, and Lillian Gish, never sat back and said "Aren't I marvellous?" They were always slogging away at their jobs; they never stopped trying to do more than they had ever done before. Jack Nicholson, Shirley MacLaine, and Paul Newman are mature contemporary actors who seem to have these characteristics. Glenn Close, Dustin Hoffman, and Robert DeNiro are somewhat younger actors with these characteristics. Their work is not always successful, but it always reveals a conscientious effort to extend their horizons, to become more than they have been before. An actor never stops working at being a richer, more resourceful actor. If he thinks he needs muscle for a role he goes to a gym; if he needs a particular accent for a character he spends the long hours necessary to acquire the accent until he's mastered it. Behind every brilliant actor there seems to be that old truth: "genius is nine parts application and hard work." Inspiration may play an important part in making an actor's work fine, but that inspiration was triggered by arduous preparation, endless effort to hone one's skills, and the willingness to find within oneself the psychological truths applicable to the role the actor is playing.

Onstage an actor can hide in a role; his characterization may be valid and yet employ qualities some distance from those central to the actor as a person. In film you cannot easily disguise your own identity in a characterization. Few actors have been able to do so, and when they have tried it has usually resulted in a hoked-up, tricky, not quite believable performance. Even more in the movies than in the theatre, the yardstick of an actor's success can be judged on whether or not he is believable in a role. It has been said that Cary Grant never played anything but Cary Grant, but in retrospect everything he played had credibility. While watching Grant on screen, the audience was totally absorbed in his characterization, whether it was in the light comedy *Bringing Up Baby,* the action drama *Gunga Din,* or the "slice-of-life" drama *None But the Lonely Heart.* Cary Grant and the character became synonymous during the picture, and it was only afterwards that the audience might say, "but he was only playing Cary Grant!"

When you watch an actor in an old film and the performance still works, it is a tribute to their acting skills. Just as clothing styles, architecture, and music go out of style, so too does the acting of many performers. From an audience point of view, what constitutes effective acting changes over the years. The interpretation of a succession of physical gestures and movement, which once was so obvious that the resultant emotion became a simple reflex, may no longer be valid. These "actions" that may have been valid at one time no longer seem acceptable to audiences. There are few actors whose work in films remains a valid human statement in later years. It's not because the actor was poor; it is because that actor was caught up in the "acting vogue" of his time. There are a handful of actors whose work remains meaningful years after the filming. Lillian Gish, for one, comes to mind. Why does her work still seem valid to contemporary audiences? Is it not because she always developed the inner life of her character so completely that you could not deny the validity of her character no matter what the current folkways and mores are that affect human behavior?

EGO AND IMAGE

One of the peculiarities of film acting is that it is best when it seems effortless. Part of this quality comes from enormous self-assurance, and there is no way that this may be imposed upon an actor. This assurance is related to ego and the actor's absolute need to think well of himself. Norma Shearer bolstered her somewhat limited talent when she said, "An actress must never lose her ego. Without it she has no talent and it is like a clock without a main stem." Many actors are rightfully accused of being egotistical or self-absorbed. However, this has little to do with self-assurance and may be the outer veneer covering up a lack of self-respect and confidence. Real self-assurance, a healthy ego, gives an actor authority and commands the audience's attention whether the actor is playing a hero, a comic character, someone despicable, someone admirable, or someone desperate. It is the kind of performance in which the audience is able to relax, knowing full well that the actor is comfortable and confident in his portrayal.

The brilliant British film actor Dirk Bogarde wrote in *Snakes and Ladders,* "Ego, for better or worse, is very much involved in this business of being an actor, because we are creatures who are obliged to use our own beings as our instrument, and we tend to have to keep reassuring ourselves—and looking for reassurance—as to how good that instrument is. It tends to make us very boring to people unless we are on constant guard against total self-preoccupation. And it has the more dangerous hazard of cutting us off from what I think is the mainspring of all good acting, which is the minute observation of one's fellow creatures who are really the fuel which feeds our attempt to create a living character." To become a fine actor, the performer must really come to know himself. Since many actors know as little about themselves as the rest of us, their own image of themselves is usually standing in the way of their acting, since it provides both limitations and prejudices. It takes a healthy ego to examine your own personality critically and yet with compassion.

It's absolutely necessary for actors to deal in the immediate use of themselves both in terms of their performing and in terms of storing up useful emotional resources drawn from their own experiences and psyche that they may be able to use in the future. Therefore, it's necessary for you to step outside your own being. Look at it coolly and assess what kind of immediate effect you are likely to make on an audience. You need to know what kind of immediate impression you make on an audience; you must realistically see yourself in the same way that the audience sees you. This means that the actor must know what kind of "image" he projects to his audience. This is far more important in film than in the theatre. Actors who are not aware of what their image is to an audience are doomed to failure, because they never understand what it is within them that an audience will accept and relate to.

Quite apart from their talent, an actor with a strong ego shares a characteristic of all successful actors; it is their tenacity—a single-mindedness, determination, or obstinacy. Actors are highly competitive. Most actors don't like the idea that they are in competition with each other; they like to think of their work as a collaborative art with everyone sharing equally in the creating of the art. In nearly all other aspects of life, however, competition is very much a part of the dynamics of life. Look at any large-sized drama department of a college or university. There you will find a highly competitive faculty all vying for promotions, campus status accomplished by the quality of their individual productions, and an ongoing effort to be the favorite professor among the students.

This condition, easy for the drama student to observe, is duplicated in nearly all business or social settings. Watch individuals compete to tell the funniest story, to be the most attractive and interesting person among their peers, to engender the admiration of their associates, to exert power over their colleagues. Michael Shurtleff in *Audition* writes, "there isn't anything for which we don't compete. Competition is healthy. Just as no game is worth the playing unless we compete, so no life activity is worth the doing unless we compete. Competition is life. Yet, most actors refuse to acknowledge this. They don't want to compete. They don't approve of the concept. And they are not therefore first-rate actors. The good actor is one who competes, willingly, who enjoys competing."

Fine actors are achievers; they want to shine, they want to prevail. It's not just for fame or the accolades, for that would be egotism. It is a burning need for achievement. To excel. It's fired by a strong ego. This need to be excellent sometimes leads actors to be ruthless and tough, but always for highly professional reasons. They are motivated by a passion for perfection.

Because actors frequently have a fragile ego and therefore have a need to think well of themselves, they tend to distort the true nature of the character they are playing. In a somewhat unconscious notion that they should make their character more sympathetic, they interpret their character as more idealistic, more humanistic, a finer human being than the script writer has conceived. The actor then sometimes uses in his personalization those elements within his own nature that he perceives as being heroic. An actor with a stronger ego can allow himself to explore the less noble aspects of his own personality in the personalization he applies to the role he is playing. He can allow himself those things within himself that are exploitive, manipulative, devious, and unattractive.

Oddly enough, there is another kind of actor who can only allow in his personalization those elements that are unattractive, perverse, far less than noble. Such actors only feel comfortable playing characters the audience cannot like. Sometimes this can be used in playing despicable characters, but to allow themselves a larger range of roles they need a stronger ego that allows them to get in touch with their likeable qualities. They may indeed know that they have a capacity for expressing feelings of love and warmth but see these qualities within themselves as openings to vulnerability. They need the kind of secure ego that can allow them to reveal their capacity for being loving and warm, generous human beings.

THINKING AND LISTENING

Alistair Cooke wrote, "In Bogart's face you could see every thought that was going on in his mind: the camera was made for his face and his face was made for the camera." The key words here are "you could see every thought." Many actors, including stars who ought to know better, don't know that the camera actually photographs thought. Sad to say it also registers the lack of thought, and this blankness shows. Only a very pretty girl at the height of her nubile powers can overcome this lack. If you don't see an actor thinking on camera (and frequently you can discern what those thoughts are) then there won't be much on the screen.

The brilliant film director, Elia Kazan, in *A Life,* writes about this unique element of film art that separates it from acting onstage. "You can—and many effective actors do—get away with faking, posturing, and indicating emotions on stage; it's difficult, if not impossible to get away with anything false before the camera. That instrument penetrates the hulk of an actor; it reveals what's truly happening—if anything, if nothing. A close-up demands absolute truth; it's a severe and awesome trial. Acting for the screen is a more honest trade." Later in his auto-biography, Kazan expands on this theme, "The camera, I concluded, is not a recording device, it's a microscope which reveals what the eye does not see. It also penetrates into a person, under the surface display, and records thoughts and feelings—whatever is going on . . . I also learned, at last, that the camera is not only a recording device but a penetrating instrument. It looks into a face, not at a face. Can this kind of effect be achieved on stage? Not nearly! A camera can even be a microscope. Linger, enlarge, analyze, study. It is a very subtle instrument, can make any face heavier, leaner, drawn, flushed, pale, jolly, depraved, saintly."

Connected to really thinking on camera is the ability to truly listen to what the other characters are saying. Listening is that special ability that only some actors have fully: the ability to really hear what the other characters are saying. And this listening is not passive but receptive in terms of what it means to your character. And you are not only listening to the words. You are hearing intonations and what the intonations imply. Sometimes the words, but more often the sound values given to the words, tell you that the other character has a hidden agenda that is pertinent to you, although they are not revealing this information to you. Sometimes their body language—and if you are truly listening then you are also truly seeing—of the other character will tell you things you need to know. He may be telling you how much he cares about your character's well-being, but his body language fairly shouts his need to exploit your character. In order to listen truly to the other characters in a scene, you must have sent out your psychological antenna ready to receive their every stated word and those thoughts beneath their words that they may wish to conceal from you.

Actions, then, are far more important than words. Actions speak for what's really going on, what's really being felt by a character. The dialog is a kind of skeleton of what's going on in a scene. The way an actor fondles a highball glass, the action that is arrested in motion as the actor's character learns something new, the way that an actor hears not only with his ears but with his eyes can help illuminate what the actor is thinking. These are examples of how an actor can externalize elements of the thought processes, but the key phrase is that the actor must truly be thinking.

If you are really thinking in character all the time, then your character will never be neutral. Your character is making discoveries, learning new things, formulating opinions, reassessing previous notions. If all this is going on in the character's thought processes, then the silent moments onscreen will be as full as the verbal moments. Your silent moments should be as full of thought and have as much point of view as your verbal moments. The camera always picks up the fact when an actor is "neutral," and that is most damaging to a performance.

Subtext is the most important thing an actor can use on film. We can see the actor thinking and making decisions more clearly and with more effectiveness on camera. Subtext is the unspoken thoughts and ideas that are running concurrently underneath the spoken lines or actions of the character. Frequently these unspoken thoughts are in direct conflict with what the character is saying or doing overtly. Al Pacino's performance in *The Godfather II* was masterful for its ability to communicate the terrible conflict going on within his character between the choices he

Al Pacino in SEA OF LOVE

Certainly one of the joys of film acting is the opportunity to concentrate totally on the truth of the moment, and this quality reaches its apogee in the close-up. The smallest gesture, the tiniest change of facial expression can reveal to the audience everything they need to know about the inner life of the character. A few actors have created such vivid, thoughtful characters that the audience actually feels that they have glimpsed the soul of the person the actor is portraying; such is the case with Al Pacino in film after film including extraordinary moments in **THE GODFATHER** series, **DOG DAY AFTERNOON,** and even in a lesser effort such as **SEA OF LOVE.** His work is always stunningly truthful.

makes for the good of the family and his personal morality. This talented actor made the subtext as relevant to his performance as anything he said out loud.

Keep in mind that the greatest moments on film have almost always been absent of dialog. They are moments when the audience, hushed and stirred, has felt that they have seen right into the very soul of the character. These moments happen when the actor is truly thinking and his thoughts and feelings register on camera.

ENERGY

We should not demand from actors that they all have the same kinds of skills and methodology. Different strokes for different folks makes sense. Good actors, however, do seem to share certain qualities of which energy is paramount. All good actors suggest external energy and, on top of that, an inner reserve of energy ready to be tapped. I remember Ethel Barrymore's great film performances in otherwise mediocre movies at the tail end of her career. At her advanced age, fighting the debilitating effects of alcoholism, she must have been frequently exhausted. Even so, her performances had great inner energy. Whenever she was onscreen, the other actors paled beside her. Behind her eyes lurked intelligence, ideas bounding, a whole inner life going on. You could see in her inner dialog surprise at what she was learning, decisions being made, a character who was constantly thinking and problem solving. "If you haven't the vitality, don't act," Laurence Olivier wrote. "An actor must be constantly vigilant about his energy, even when he is young and he thinks his body can take every abuse. The body is a vital part of the equipment. I used to keep fit—best for the movement, the gestures . . . the vitality doesn't disappear altogether, of course, that would be the end of life. You have to nurse it."

When you watch movies from the forties and fifties, they are often amusing for their naivete and the simplicity of the scripted characters, but much of the acting had great energy. Many of the directors then came from the theatre so they knew how to pace a scene, vary rhythms, allow the actors the space to play off each other. The scenes were not cut as tightly as today, which made it possible for the actors to build energy

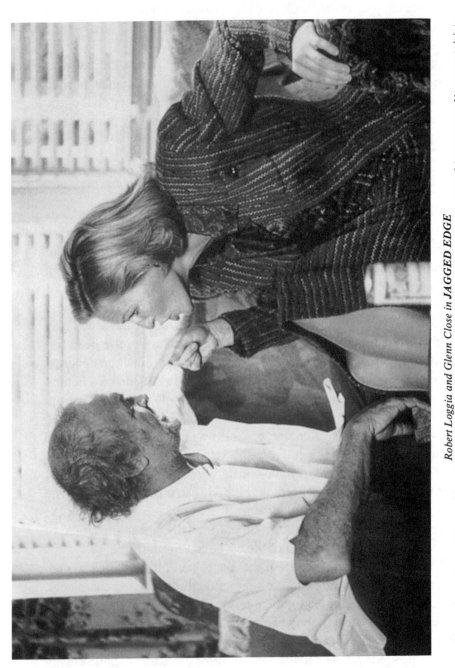

Robert Loggia and Glenn Close in JAGGED EDGE

Actors who have a kind of kinetic energy always are attractive; the audience feels as though it can catch some of that energy and incorporate it into themselves. The kinetic energy of Bette Davis lighting a cigarette, James Cagney jauntily strutting down a street, Al Pacino, a whirlwind of action in *Dog Day Afternoon*, and of Glenn Close in *Fatal Attraction*, *Jagged Edge*, and *Les Liaisons Dangereuses*—even in repose she emanates energy.

into a sustained scene. I think one of the unspoken reasons that films currently are cut so quickly from shot to shot is that the directors and editors know that the scenes lack energy so that they work overtime to regain that energy by fast cuts and a pulsating sound track. Fast cuts aren't so much a concession to a pop-video, MTV-influenced audience with a limited attention span as it is an attempted solution to getting energy into what would otherwise be a painfully slow show. More of that energy, however, should come from the actors. Joan Blondell, one of the great comediennes in films of the thirties and forties, lamented this lack of energy. "When I go to the movies . . . I see such restraint, such blank pusses (faces), that I wonder if these actors know what they're doing. There's a very fine line between underacting and not acting at all. And not acting is what lots of actors are guilty of.

TRUSTING YOUR INSTINCTS

"I love Bette Davis because she's not afraid to be bad. When Bette's good, she's real good. When she's bad, she's awful . . . but at least she's not afraid to bat an eyelash." That marvellous quote is from Shelley Winters, and it reinforces my notion that fine actors trust themselves and their instincts; they are never afraid to take risks.

You've really got to go with your instincts to be an outstanding film actor. It's all you have to go on, really. The reason there aren't many good actors is because there are few people who have that deep-seated confidence in their intuitions. There's no way to analyze some things. If you are watching actors doing a scene onscreen, you have to ask yourself, "Is it right or isn't it right?" You can't analyze it. Either you've got to know in your heart that it's right or that it's wrong. You can't always know why it's wrong, but if it feels wrong then you've got to trust yourself to try something else.

Film actors must be good at adapting to new situations, different ways of playing a scene than the way they originally saw it. They must be able to make these adjustments quickly and they must be able to change their character's choice making in the scene not mechanically but in some kind of way that is true and valid. Adapting to unexpected circumstances (a different set, a different kind of acting partner than expected, a different time frame than was originally planned) and still keeping the character valid is a major task of the film actor.

The film actor must learn to trust the wild inconsistency of human behavior. If people are full of surprises and seem "out of character" with some of the choices they make, then this inconsistency can sometimes be used in an actor's characterization. People are always full of surprises. We even surprise ourselves by the sudden unexpected choices we make and the actions we sometimes take. We can't quite believe what we are doing, but any psychologist will quickly explain that these choice-making surprises were already within us, lurking in our unconscious, waiting for the appropriate moment to surface. If this is true of ourselves, and surely you must admit that you have sometimes surprised yourself with your choices, decisions, and impulsive things you have done, then it is certainly true in the characters we play. Allow the audience to be surprised by doing the unexpected—so long as those unexpected choices aren't bizarre but could actually spring from the character's being. Interesting acting always includes this element of the unpredictable in it. Good actors are always full of surprises; we never quite know what they're going to do next.

This is the age of underacting. It's been a long time now since nineteenth-century overacting, and yet actors do not trust strong emotional feelings for fear that they will be overacting. On the basis of much of the acting we see, if this kind of acting had caloric value, audiences would die of malnutrition. Actors are so fearful of being melodramatic that they choose to flatten out all their feelings, to wash out the tensions, hurts, fears, doubts, romantic flurries that flutter their hearts. It drives me crazy when actors refuse to play a scene to the hilt. Everyone is so afraid of overacting that nearly everything is underplayed. It's as dishonest for its understatement as nineteenth-century acting was dishonest for its overstatement.

Out of fear that they will not be able to build to the scene's high point, actors hold back. Holding back is a form of dishonesty. People don't hold back in life; they simply experience the feeling appropriate to the moment and actors must do the same thing. They're fearful that they won't be able to make the peaks of emotional fervor called for later in the scene if they start too high. Nonsense. If you make a full emotional commitment to what your character is experiencing, you will be able to go wherever it's natural for your character to take you. You don't need to do anything so arbitrary as modulating your character's experience so that you can build to an emotional climax later. If you doubt me, look carefully at the great scenes in films. A good starter would be to inspect Marlon Brando's performance in *Last Tango in Paris,* in the scene in which he pours out all the anguish and fury he feels about his failed marriage to his dead wife as she lies in her coffin. He starts at white heat and the scene becomes ever more powerful by the moment. Brando holds nothing back from the moment the camera turns and the result is one of the most searingly honest, revelatory scenes ever seen on the screen. That took trust. Trust on Brando's part and trust on director Bertolucci's part. Something of the same risk taking can be seen in Al Pacino's work in *Dog Day Afternoon.* He doesn't try to put a heavy lid of control on his work in this movie; he trusts his intuitions, and the energy and commitment to each moment builds your excitement in watching him moment by moment.

Actor-director Charles Haid subscribes to the same notion. "Although I am aware of the connective moments from scene to scene and how they are influential to each other, I think it's easier to play for the moment." By this Haid is referring to what Harold Clurman always told his actors, "deal with each moment in time for its own value." Haid continues, "You can prepare for the role and have a pretty good idea of what you want to achieve in a scene but, when you actually come to the shooting of that moment in the film, you've got to be able to change it if that's appropriate. You've got to be free to change the shape of what you are doing because sometimes the most amazing things happen in terms of spontaneity and you should trust whatever that spontaneous response is and go for it. You have to be afraid of rigidity, of not trusting those impulses. After awhile you see that some of the best actors are very eccentric; usually the reason they seem to be so eccentric is because they are very free and they know who they are. What I am trying to say is that the part of yourself that is most alive is that part of you that is going to be most suspect in the minds of others."

As vastly different as each role he plays is, what makes Dustin Hoffman's work so effective onscreen is that he trusts himself suf-

*Marlon Brando in **LAST TANGO IN PARIS***
Actors in film soon learn that their most effective moments are silent. They discover that the body language they employ in creating a character can sometimes be the thing audiences remember years after having seen the movie.

ficiently to take a human being's private world and make it public. From *The Graduate* to *Midnight Cowboy* to *Tootsie,* he has managed to get beneath the skin of his characters—usually individuals who wish to keep hidden their desires, fears, and hopes. Even though his characters value their privacy, and Hoffman plays these characters accordingly, he has the ability to communicate the inner life of the character to the audience. His characters clearly want to keep hidden their private lives, but the actor makes their lives public. There have to be various parts of Hoffman's psyche that are appropriate for the diverse characters he plays; as with all great actors he is able to make his private world public, and it is this risk-taking ability that separates the good actor from the bad actor. Hoffman has given himself permission to be ridiculous, stripped naked of the character camouflage that most of us use to protect ourselves.

The trouble with far too many actors in current films is that they are controlling their performances before they have any significant emotional experience and commitment to the moment worth controlling. They need to trust their feelings and intuitions. They can start by looking for the warmth in the characters they are playing that will interest us. Add to that the character's humor, romantic expectations, and dreams, since often those are the elements most important to us in our own lives. All these qualities are possible in many scripts and yet often the actor leaves them out. Why make cold choices when you can make romantic choices? For that matter, who cares about actors who seem to find only the negative qualities in a character they are playing? Trust yourself.

HUMOR

It's a human characteristic to try to find the humor in all situations; if we didn't find humor sometimes life would become intolerable. I remember my family gathering at my parents' home following the funeral of my father. All the uncles and aunts, all our nephews and nieces, and most especially the grieving widow, my mother, were there. Our father had been dearly loved by a great many people and he was highly respected. To relieve tension, drinks were passed around to everyone and, in truth, everyone drank more than they ordinarily would. It loosened tongues and revived flagging spirits and soon we were joyously remembering our father and retelling stories of the funny things that had happened between him and the rest of the family. We recalled him happily and without sorrow. Remembering funny anecdotes and ridiculous experiences together, the employment of humor did not lessen the love we felt for our father. Our humor celebrated his life.

The generous drinks that led our family memories to turn to humor are a natural part of the life process. Indeed, the happy memories recalled at a time of sorrow are part of the healing process. But actors forget this very human need to find humor at times of travail. They take humor out of the situation instead of putting it in. In their search for being truthful, they have mistakenly done the exact opposite from what is true in life. When playing in serious dramas, the actors should always look for the opposite side of the coin, the moments of humor. The seriousness will take care of itself. Conversely, in playing in a comedy, actors should look for what is serious in their character to help give that character dimension and humanness.

Young actors sometimes equate being downhearted, somewhat glum, and humorless with being serious actors. Nothing could be more counter-productive to their success as actors. Difficulty in putting humor into their acting results in their playing one-dimensional characters, people whom the audience finds colorless, boring, and far from truthful, counter to the intended goal of the serious actor. Actors must look for the humor in their characters; if it's not there, then the actor must find a way of putting it there. It's human not to like people who take themselves too seriously; you must be cautioned not to play your character without a sense of humor unless you want the audience actively to dislike you.

AFFIRMING LIFE

People respond warmly and with enthusiasm to life-affirming characters; they pull away from life-negating people. Why then is it so common for actors to make negative choices? In playing a scene, actors almost automatically move towards the negative choices that a character might make in a situation; they fail to recognize that the character just as truthfully might make a positive choice. Why is it not just as valid for the character to see the cup as half full as it is to see the cup as half empty? It's as though most actors just ordinarily gravitate toward a "downer's" attitude. Do we like such negative people in life? Sometimes in life negative choices are thrust upon us, but it is not something most people would willingly take upon themselves. If we are life-affirming people, we work positively to overcome the negative circumstances in our lives. When observing people, we admire those who do not succumb to the troubles they confront but work hard to overcome those troubles. When playing a character, then, an actor should see that negative choices are probably only one side of his character. The actor should look for what motivates the character: dreams, hopes, wishes, romance. Most of us dream of a better life for ourselves, for happiness in our careers and, more importantly, in our love life. When an actor leaves out of any scene his character's hopes and dreams, he leaves out the best part of the character he should be playing.

ROLE-PLAYING IN LIFE

People play games in life; they are often caught up in a bit of role-playing in their relationships with bosses, colleagues, family, and lovers. Yet actors want immediately to eliminate that very natural human characteristic from the people they play. A psychologist even named his book *Games People Play,* and yet actors refuse to see that what their script is trying to tell them: your character is role-playing. Actors don't trust the fact that every day in life people are often role-playing. Watch a young romantic couple on the beach. He looks for physical activities that can suggest his maleness. He takes mock stances, strikes bravado poses, and plays the knight in shining armor. She reacts with heightened femininity; she pretends to be helpless and dependent. She plays the princess who needs to be saved by the hero. This is rather obvious role-playing, but we play many different roles in relationships to such different kinds of people in our lives as our boss, our parents, our children, our romantic partner. If this is so in life then it should also be so in the roles we play on film.

Look for the role-playing that is going on between people in a scene. Woody Allen's films are filled with such people, as is demonstrated in the scene from *Manhattan* that is printed later in this book.

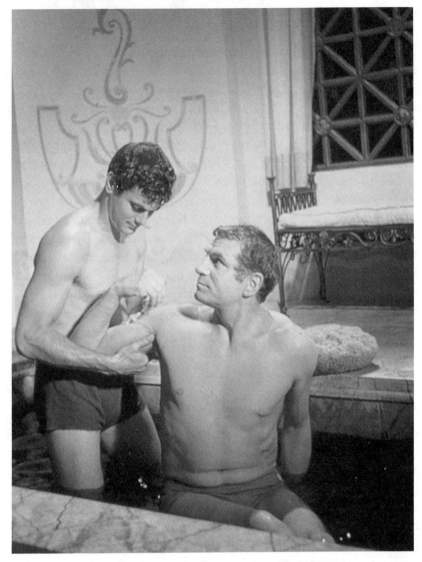

Laurence Olivier, often hailed as the greatest actor of the 20th century, personifies the British actor while Tony Curtis certainly is representative of an American style of acting. They are seen here in a sequence from **SPARTACUS.**

British actors have a very different kind of training than American actors. With few exceptions they are not exposed to the "method" school of acting, which is an outgrowth of the system of acting developed by Constantin Stanislavsky at the Moscow Art Theatre. In their leading drama schools, such as the Royal Academy of Dramatic Art and the Central School of Speech and Drama, the emphasis is on developing their voices, learning how to handle the language of Shakespeare and the classics, and moving in a more stylized, grander manner than their American counterparts. The result of these differences in dramatic training is that American actors are frequently more creditable in realistic, natural settings while the British actors excel in playing larger-than-life characters.

Another scene included in our text, *Boys and Girls Together,* reveals both humorously and poignantly the role-playing and games people play as a couple explore and fear the significance of their falling in love.

Think back to all the romantic comedies the young Katharine Hepburn played opposite James Stewart, Cary Grant, and later Spencer Tracy. Her characters were always role-playing a bit. Often she was a wealthy young heiress who tripped over the traces of propriety; she seemed to defy the conventional morality around her. Underneath this role-playing, we glimpsed a fine young woman who was caring, sometimes vulnerable, and always sensitive to other people's feelings. In all the films, her character was a deep believer in romantic love. Part of the joy of watching Katharine Hepburn was our knowledge that her character was role-playing.

Actors then must come to trust that their characters are sometimes role-playing and reveal this in their performances. This will certainly not make their characterization less honest. The characters choose to play the right game at the right time in the right place just as people do in life. Most of us accommodate the people in our lives with a certain amount of role playing. When I'm with my brother-in-law and his family, all sports lovers, I take a greater interest in spectator sports than I ordinarily would. I play the role of avid sports fan. It makes me fit into their world more comfortably as much for them as for me. When I am with fellow faculty members I assume the role of professor and more often than not linger longer in a conversation on education than I would choose to do on my own. Professors love to play the role of academician and, believe me, most of it is role-playing.

Actors must look for the role-playing, that their character does. American actors sometimes wonder why British actors often get the juicy, larger-than-life character roles. Well, think about it. Because the British actors seem to know that their characters are role-playing, they trust themselves to take on the size and style that go with such role-playing. Often it has a quality of self-mockery in it, which is something I think lots of people in life have when they are role-playing. British actors trust their characters to sometimes make self-mocking, devious, out-of-proportion reactions to situations because they know their characters would do so in such circumstances.

Robert DeNiro and Kevin Costner in THE UNTOUCHABLES.
Sometimes less is more in the art of film acting. No one personifies this better than Clint Eastwood and Steve McQueen, whose films have always kept talk to a minimum. The audience is allowed to fill in the silence with their own fantasy needs and thoughts through the persona of the actor; they imagine what he's thinking and feeling in terms of their own thoughts and feelings. While this appears to be minimalist acting, other performers using the same approach have experienced dismal failure. Kevin Costner in most of his films has used this minimalist approach by communicating that he is a feeling, concerned, involved person who finds it difficult to reveal emotions outwardly. It represents a contrast in style from the volatile approach of Robert DeNiro.

An American actor who knew this intuitively and did it continually in his film work was Buster Keaton. There was always an element of role-playing in his film character: the stoic bravery in the face of over-whelming odds, the matter-of-fact courage he would display in front of the woman he loved, the refusal to accept defeat against incredible obstacles. All of this was done with just a hint of self-mockery at the chivalrous attitudes of his character. He always played his character as though he knew he was out of synch with a more pragmatic world.

Peter O'Toole has revived a flagging career by playing gallant ruins who have nearly destroyed their lives foolishly with too much excess in drinking, loving, and dreaming. His characters seem to step back from themselves, see the havoc they have brought upon themselves, laugh at their own follies, and get on with their lives. Both the characters and O'Toole are role-playing.

Sometimes actors forget that the actor must always know more than the characters they're playing. Since characters, like people in every-day life, role-play, it is necessary that the actor know that the person he is playing may have these characteristics. How else can the actor suggest the kind of deceits that characters play on themselves, the fantasies that they allow themselves as characters? Deceits and fan-tasies are qualities in a person that the character may not know about himself but that the actor playing the character must know in order to be insightful in the choices that the character makes. For example, a young man may think he despises a young woman when, in truth, he harbors romantic feelings for her. What is going on in the "unconscious" of the character must be consciously understood by the actor playing the character. We all know what it is to lie to ourselves, to rationalize certain actions we take, to justify ourselves sometimes for actions we take, when what we really want is quite the opposite from our overt action; the same thing is true for the characters we play. The characters we play on camera are no more straightforward than we ourselves are in life.

SUMMATION

A characteristic of many good film actors is that they can be very quiet, very still; they seem to be able to incorporate a character and then let it come out easily, naturally, as if it had always been in them. These qualities are the result of a strong ego, appropriate energy, the ability to reveal thinking and listening on camera, and perhaps most of all, an ability to trust and use their instincts. They never use three gestures when one is sufficient. They know that if they have completely surrendered to their character's being, all of this will communicate itself on camera. Such actors suggest that the inner life of the character is at least as strong as the external life of the character. An audience need not know what the character is experiencing in his inner life so long as they believe that the inner life is rich and completely experienced. Indeed, some of the excitement of a superlative performance lies in our not questioning any of it; we simply accept that the character has many dimensions of which we are privy to only a few.

Good film actors never depend on words as the primary means of projecting what their character is experiencing. They recognize that it is in their choices of activities and in their eyes that the camera, and hence the audience, will know what the character is experiencing.

Good film actors remember that film is a visual medium. To be remembered, you've got to be a visual performer. When you really come down to it, what you remember about one of film's best actresses, Bette Davis, is how she lights a cigarette and then smokes it—those savage, hasty puffs, her kinetic energy. What she does is much more important than what she says.

Good film actors remember that acting onstage is communicating with a group; acting on camera is communication with one other person. The camera is a surrogate for that one person watching the actor whether that person is sitting in a crowded movie theatre or watching in front of the television set. This intimate exchange between one actor and one person in the audience is unique to film acting. Some very fine actors have described their love affair with the camera; whether consciously or not, such actors have come to see that the camera represents that one person out there with whom they are sharing the emotional experience and the life of the character.

CHAPTER 4

THE ACTOR
AND THE DIRECTOR

A good director has no desire to be Svengali to the actor's Trilby. Yet there is often a kind of uneasiness in the relationship between actors and directors. Both want the other to like them and both feel an enormous pressure mostly induced by the economics of the business; each hour of filming costs between $5,000 and $10,000, and those staggering figures never are far from the consciousness of both performer and director.

One of the joys of working in the theatre is the long hours spent rehearsing. Both actor and director have the luxury of time, which allows them to explore all the nuances of character and how that character serves the spine of the script. No such luck on camera. Those mounting costs force both actor and director always to work against the clock, to get the scene done quickly and, they hope, right the first time.

So much of the director's time is consumed with other aspects of production that he is perforce unable to give as much time to the actor as desired. His work day is overwhelming; it frequently includes consultations with the cinematographer, art director, production manager, producer. It may include hasty trips to scout out a new location when a previously chosen site becomes unusable. The director has almost as many elements pulling at him during a day's shoot as a general has in conducting a war.

Well-known character actor Ned Beatty has said, "You have to be slightly mad to want to be a director. There has to be an area of masochism in your personality. It's a leadership position and people will approach it from every way you can think of. Some directors just get shoved aside and told not to get in the way. I can't tell you how many times I've seen that happen. Actors are very powerful. Once directors have two weeks of film on an actor, the actor becomes damn near omnipotent." Imagine what it must be to try to guide an actor whose box office potency is strong: By the time the director gets around to working with an actor in a smaller role, his energies have already been taxed to the limit.

How can you help make the director's job easier? Be prepared. Arrive on the set with a clear understanding of your character's objective. Make an educated guess as to the spine of the script. This isn't so easy when you consider that many television scripts are paste-up jobs and have no spine. Determine what your character's relationship is to the other characters in the screenplay. Needless to say, arrive on the set with your dialog word perfect. Any actor will occasionally blow lines, but to be consistently shaky in knowing your dialog is unforgivable.

What surprises actors new to film is that good film directing frequently has a unique quality: that of never saying a word if a gesture or an indication would help in itself, never using one word more than is necessary to indicate what is wanted. When William Hurt was asked what did he need from a director, his reply was, "Sanction. That implies so much, because it implies understanding of my craft, of my need to do something I've never done before, as well as the permission to attempt . . . to sanction my childish courage—childlike courage, really."

British actor Dirk Bogarde, who has worked with Luchino Visconti, Joseph Losey, Rainer Werner Fassbinder and some of the world's greatest film directors, talks about Losey in his book *Snakes and Ladders*. "Like all the greatest directors, Losey never tells one what to do or how to do it. Ever. Only what not to do. Which is very different. You give him your character and he will watch it develop, encouraging or modifying, always taking what is offered and using it deftly. . . . There is no waste of chatter, no great in-depth discussions about motivation, no mumbo-jumbo about identification, soul, or truth."

Time constrictions in shooting schedules often wreak havoc in the relationship between directors and actors. One of the problems is that most young actors feel it is an insult to their intelligence and/or creativity if the director spells out exactly what he wants the actor to do with a role. More disturbing is when a director gives an actor a line reading if he feels that the actor is not quite grasping what should happen in a scene. Most of the time the actor is correct to want to find his own organic reading of a speech since it's part of his total characterization and, presumably, he has a sense of what the total characterization should be. On the other hand, it can also be assumed that the director understands the larger design of the script, has determined what the spine of the script is, and how all the elements of the performances must serve that larger purpose.

With each moment on the set eating up huge sums of money, the director sometimes fails to understand that to be successful, the actor must be more than a puppet parroting lines. The actor feels that if he is being given a line reading, it is an intrusion on his interpretation and perhaps even a distortion of the truth of his vision. If a director gives the actor a reading, the actor may scream that he doesn't want to hear it. The actor, however, needs to remember that the director giving the line reading may be prompted exclusively by his need to get the film shot quickly in order to keep inside the budget; there just may not be enough time for a more sophisticated but time-consuming working out of the vocal interpretation.

Every once in a while you meet an actor, however, who is so confident in his own talent—Tony Perkins and Laurence Olivier are examples—that they can listen to any suggestions, any variations in interpretation and make use of them if they want to. That's real professionalism.

Most gifted directors prefer not to tell the actor what to do or how to do it. If they do tell the actor how to interpret a sequence, it's usually a matter of expediency. More frequently the fine director reveals his worth in telling you what not to do. You give him your character and he only speaks to you if he feels that your interpretation works against the intent of the character and the screenplay. If the actor hears little in the way of suggestions from the director, it is well to remember that he was cast for the qualities that he already has in his persona. It's very likely that the producers and director chose this particular actor because they know the kind of choices he will make in his characterization and those are the choices they want.

For some actors who are new to films, it comes as a surprise to learn that there are directors with very fine reputations who have little to say to actors that is valuable. It's not that they don't value the actor, but that they really don't know what to say to an actor that can be helpful. Their training for motion pictures did not prepare them for helping the actor to blossom in his characterization. Such directors may have a great conceptual sense or a great visual sense so that what they put into each frame is brilliant. They may be able to tell a story cinematically in ways that are breathtaking, but they will have nothing of value to help an actor in his performance. Robert Redford spoke about this problem: "I'm less comfortable with some of the younger directors because I don't think they have as much understanding of performing as they do of the technical end of things. I understand what they're saying intellectually, and I say 'Yes, I get it.' But their ability to inspire you is really not that great. When you're with a director that you really trust, you let yourself go more easily. But if you feel you have someone who can't talk to actors, then you say, 'Well, I think I know more about this person, so I'd better protect myself.' I'm not just going to indiscriminately do what he says . . . there are many directors I've worked with who seem frightened of actors. And that's too bad, because actors help the creative process enormously. But very often I've worked with directors who felt they needed to be tough. So even when they didn't know, they would say, 'do it! Do this!' And you knew they didn't have any conviction about it."

Directors who realize they have little to contribute to an actor's performance are smart when they solve this weakness through their casting. They know when they cast a film that the actors they choose have personas exactly right for the film. John Ford was certainly one of the finest directors in the history of motion pictures, but he had very little to say to actors that would be of help to them. Cecil B. De Mille used to hire dialog directors because he didn't have a clue as to what to tell an actor that would enhance a performance. Yet, these directors deserved their fame and stature in the business. There are many such directors in films today, people who came up from editing, or cinematography, or screen writing. They are genuinely gifted directors except for their limited knowledge of the actors' craft and the ways in which an actor enriches their performance. Since this is a reality of the business, it is important for the actor to bring his own preparation to the role and not expect assistance from the director. Furthermore, once you understand a director's working methods, it's foolish to ask the director questions that may intimidate him or make him aware of his limitations in working with actors.

We look at directors whose reputations have been built on their cinematic eye. What is their Achilles' heel? Their lack of knowledge of what their primary tool, the actor, must do. They tend to give such obvious directing suggestions as "say it louder here," or "move the scene along faster." A splendid filmmaker such as Stanley Kubrick has made several seriously flawed films in recent years. One of the reasons for this is that he has nothing to say to an actor; he's failed to compensate for this limitation in his casting and has often used actors of very limited skills, and their wan performances dilute the quality of the film. Sometimes his films seem bloodless because the actor is not sufficiently valued.

Jack Nicholson is a very fine actor, but he needs directors who know what to do with him and how to use him. He never needs directors to tell him what to do, but sometimes he needs directors to tell him what not to do. In Kubrick's *The Shining,* his way-over-the-top performance was admirable for its risk taking, but it was a performance which, even kindly, must be described as bizarre. Nicholson desperately needed the objective
eye of a director to help shape what potentially could have been a brilliant performance.

Even so, you have to keep in mind that, "You really can't judge yourself as clearly as the director can," as Michael Caine tells us in his book *Acting in Film.* "His perception will usually prove sounder than your instinct. Anyway, he's the boss, and you might as well trust him. Some actors can't give in, can't compromise. If you're an actor new to film, I suggest you let the director direct and get on with your job: following his direction."

Keep in mind, however, that it is your face that's up there on the screen. You can't tell the audience that you didn't have sufficient help from the director. You must have developed your craft of acting and have prepared yourself sufficiently for the role you are doing so that your performance will be good with or without any help from the director.

When the director does talk to you, or even better, with you, give him all your attention. Really listen! He may not necessarily have the actors' language that is familiar to you from actors' workshops and acting classes, but you can still benefit by looking for the full implication of what he is after. He might say "speed it up here" when what he really means is that he wants you to act more spirited with a kind of bravado that he thinks appropriate for the character. You must look beyond such directorial words as "talk slower here" to find their real significance. Perhaps he means that your character is tentative, uncertain of himself in the situation, trying to figure out what to do. Look for the full implication of what the director is seeking.

There are some directors who are wonderful with actors and are of enormous benefit to them. The two Sidneys—Lumet and Pollack—come to mind. Their stage backgrounds have assisted them in knowing how to communicate with actors. When you get such a director, that's a plus but it is by no means the norm.

When a director is giving you suggestions, keep your mind open to his ideas. For God's sake don't waste time defending yourself or explaining away why you are doing what you are doing. Listen carefully to the director and try as much as you can to adapt your characterization to his ideas. Don't make the director have to stop you and ask for the same things over and over in take after take. After a while, the director will give up and settle for what you give him, but you can be assured that you will never work on any of his projects again.

Some actors end up in an adversarial relationship with their directors. This is all right if you are a star and the final arbiter of what ends up in the frame. If you are not in such an exalted position, then it is wise to adapt yourself to what the director wants. The director really does want you to give the best performance possible, and he is only interested in your performance. When he is trying to communicate ideas to you, listen! Don't reveal what a clever person you are by anticipating the ends of his sentences; let him finish his ideas and if you understand what he is saying give him some indication of your understanding. If you have an honest difference of opinion that you feel is central to the moment's effectiveness on screen, decide whether the conditions of the production warrant your asking more questions or expressing your views. If the production is for television and on a back-breaking schedule that cannot afford the luxury of discussion, accept this reality and get on with shooting the scene. If this is a major film production with a more expansive schedule and a larger budget that makes possible finer distinctions in characterizing, then you may want to take the time to discuss the scene.

When you are on the set and the scene is ready to be shot, this is no time for you to need to define every beat and aspect of the script. You should have done everything you can to prepare yourself for this scene before the day's shooting began. Don't intellectualize your work as you are doing it. Some actors, in a misguided notion of how to make each moment truthful, analyze every choice they make searching for the justification; they stand outside the character evaluating the truthfulness of their behavior and, because they are standing outside the character, they do not become the character. They intellectually become a truthful character but the audience doesn't believe them. The actor must throw away his intellectualizing at that very moment when the director calls "Action!"

An example of this can be seen in the work of Mickey Rourke and Eric Roberts in *The Pope of Greenwich Village*. Both of these actors are capable of fine work, but in this movie, as *New Yorker* critic Pauline Kael pointed out, "these actors do not so much act as show off, doing shallow acting class set pieces that may impress the hell out of each other but do not have a chance of connecting with or moving an audience."

Actors, quite rightfully in the face of certain evidence, are wary of directors. They've all heard the oft-quoted producers' remark that "the lunatics have taken over the asylum" that accompanied the creation of United Artists Pictures by a group of actors. This disparaging of actors continued when Alfred Hitchcock described actors as "cattle." The celebrated suspense director was really speaking only for the press. It was a smart-ass remark that made good copy for the newspapers. When Alfred Hitchcock described actors as "cattle," he was expressing a view shared by many movie people who are not performers; it's a misguided contempt and perhaps an unconscious expression of envy on the part of people who recognize that acting is as much fun as it is work.

Hitchcock was really speaking for the newspapers; he knew that such a jibe made good copy and would help sell tickets to his films. But Hitchcock almost always cast his films with actors who were capable and who could successfully play the roles they were given. An indication of how Hitchcock valued actors can be seen in the meticulous casting of the smaller roles; from his early British films to nearly the end of his career, Hitchcock chose actors who regardless of the size of their roles gave colorful and interesting performances. In truth, Hitchcock by his actions, by his casting, revealed that he saw actors as much more than cattle.

Actors mustn't fear directors. They aren't the enemy, although some actors seem to think so. Whatever bad experiences these actors had in their formative years with the so-called authority figures in their lives, these negative experiences mustn't be transferred to their relationship to directors. A director wants the same thing you do: a fine performance. If the director has any skill at all, he can serve as a kind of audience for the actor, and audiences can be very helpful. The director, at his best, is an intelligent and educated audience.

Even if his experience does not include any knowledge of the actors' craft, at least he can be an intelligent audience and, therefore, helpful to the actor on that level. Unfortunately, since many directors don't know how to talk to actors, the actors become jaded about directors and believe they are not much more than traffic cops. An actor and his director should be in close communication; the actor should trust the director and the director should trust the actor.

Finally, since directors are frequently so busy with a thousand technical things and do not have the time to talk to the actor, the actor can very quietly inquire of the cameraman, "What is the framing of this scene?" If you can learn what is in the camera frame it sometimes can assist you in choosing what to do in the scene. Some directors feel that it should not concern the actor what appears in the frame, but I think this knowledge is very helpful in your choice making. For example, if you have appeared in the preceding scene of the script in a medium-long shot in which you concluded the sequence with a certain action, then it is useful to you as an actor in the next sequence, a medium-close shot, to pick up the continuation of that same physicalization and carry it into the shot. It gives your performance an added charge, a kind of excitement which is the sort of physical tying together that editors look for when they are cutting a film from sequence to sequence.

Whatever conditions prevail on the set, the actor should look for any guidelines that can be helpful. You may have waited in makeup and costume for five hours before they get to your scene. But then, if you are a good actor, you have firmly established your prior actions just before this scene commences, you remember where you came from and why, and you somehow find fresh energy to bring to the scene. If you are smart, you have kept the avenues of conversation open between you and the director.

Directors talk to other directors, and if their experience with you has been a happy one, it's likely that that information will be passed on to their colleagues. It's human to be annoyed by an arrogant director, but work hard to keep yourself objective and open to the possibilities in a role. Perhaps there are things in his suggestions that you can use. Look for them and try to translate those ideas into actions that will work for the scene. Woo the director with friendliness and openness to his ideas; it may result in your giving a better performance than you had hoped for. Furthermore, he'll remember you the next time he's casting.

CHAPTER 5

STARDOM

Young acting students dream of stardom. They never admit to such hopes and dreams but often that is their secret desire. Stardom is an elusive thing to obtain and even more elusive to describe. Why does one actor become a star and another not? Charisma? Good looks? Presence? A kind of authority that puts an audience in awe?

The purpose of this chapter is to describe some of the factors that help make some actors stars and to discourage young actors from concerning themselves with that elusive goal.

Stardom is more often than not the actor's getting the right role at the right moment in life and that role then takes him to stardom. Nearly every famous actor can name a specific role that catapulted their career into stardom. Would Jack Nicholson have become a star were it not for the magic combination of a quirky, unusual character and a script that its young audience believed was their personal history in *Easy Rider?* Would that leap into the public's eye have been solidified were it not for his next film, *Five Easy Pieces,* in which his intelligent, alienated character seemed to be at odds with the overwhelming "establishment"? Moviegoers identified so strongly with his alienation that each audience member believed he was speaking directly to their personal dilemma in a depersonalized society. Jack Nicholson became a kind of spokesman for the sixties' generation. Given his unique qualities as an actor he

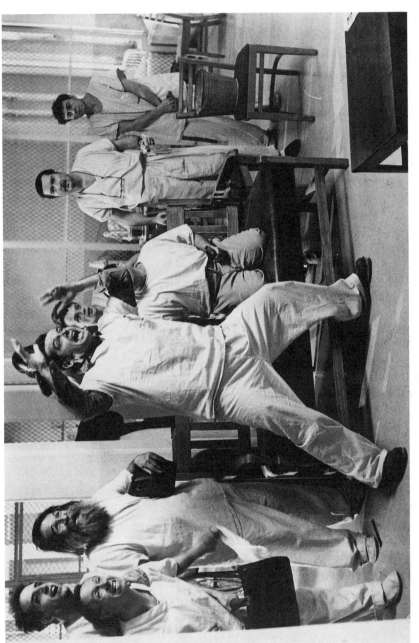

Jack Nicholson in ONE FLEW OVER THE CUCKOO'S NEST

Audiences the world over have liked that independence of spirit so often epitomized by American actors in the movies; from the early years of motion pictures to the present they have identified and empathized with the non-conformist, the rebel, the guy listening to his own drummer. Jack Nicholson, who represents a person of such spirit, explains, "I've never let anyone think they own me." Brando, McQueen, Gable, and Kirk Douglas all have made their careers playing such characters.

would undoubtedly have been a successful working actor but probably not a star if he had lived as a young actor in another generation.

Nicholson recognizes this himself. "A star is not a manipulated image," he said. "Only that audience out there makes a star. It's up to them. You can't do anything about it, or I never would've got anywhere. Stars would all be Louis B. Mayer's cousins if you could make 'em up."

Gary Cooper epitomized stardom in the thirties and forties and, while he was never more than a merely adequate actor though an extremely handsome one, he represented the fantasy needs of his generation and therefore became a star. If you were to compare his skills with those of Henry Fonda, a product of the same generation, you would quickly see that Fonda was a superior actor and yet, arguably, Cooper was a bigger star. Why?

Cooper was described as the strong, silent type and with good reason. If Cooper had to utter more than three sentences sequentially, it became evident that his handling of dialog was leaden. Yet Cooper's strong, silent type represented the kind of man whose inarticulate feelings of psychological pain coupled with courage was the lot of so many depression-era men. *Meet John Doe* and *Mr. Deeds Goes to Town* gave Cooper roles that epitomized the average man of his generation: decent, patriotic, both strong and gentle, stammering a kind of half-formed, embarrassed idealism. He became the symbol for the way his generation wished to believe itself to be.

In the last couple of decades the actor whose work most closely resembles Gary Cooper's is Clint Eastwood. His early television cowboy roles moved him towards stardom, and when he graduated into film westerns and action thrillers, his stardom was assured. What Eastwood represents on screen most of all is the disenfranchised man of the seventies and eighties who feels that society is outside of his control and who feels that he is a pawn in some giant conspiracy among big government, big business, and the intellectuals. For the blue-collar worker of the seventies and eighties who has watched his job opportunities fading away, while at the same time he has been given the impression that his contribution to society is not valued, Eastwood's character strikes a deep, responsive chord. Blue-collar workers are frequently people who excel in physical action but are less effective in cognitive reasoning. Eastwood's characters fulfill their emotional needs in that his heroic figures settle their problems with action, fists, and guns. Often Eastwood's movie adversaries are clever, manipulating men who are, however, without scruples. It is easy to identify with the Eastwood characters who are usually men of good will but are outsiders in a complicated society; they solve their problems through physical action. Eastwood, unquestionably a better director than actor, has understood his audience, so his films reflect the fantasy needs of his fans. The rugged star said, "I see my films as first aid to the modern male psyche. Masculinity is becoming obsolete. Most jobs today can be held by women. Many men have become defensive and enjoy being taken to another time, another period, where masculinity was important to survival."

Someone of quite different style, English actor Dirk Bogarde, was brought to Hollywood to play the leads in several films. Bogarde has had a distinguished career working with some of the world's finest directors, including Joseph Losey and Luchino Visconti. In his book *Snakes and Ladders,* Bogarde describes a conversation he had with a tough publicist about a big-budget Hollywood picture that Bogarde felt was not going well. Bogarde asked, "and if it fails at the box office?"

"You'll fail, too," the publicist answered. "Remember this, honey; it isn't great acting that gets you up there as a star, it's great box office grosses. Nothing more and nothing less. That chestnut about being only as good as your last movie is absolutely true. Absolutely. If this movie makes it you'll be offered every role from Mary Magdalene to Stalin—never mind you don't look like them; they'll fix it so you do because you'll be bankable, they can sell you. When you don't sell, they don't buy, not the Producers, not the Exhibitors, not the goddamned audiences. Maybe one near miss is allowable, but two is curtains. Box Office equals Big Names equals Bankability; anything else equals Bankrupt."

The money men of Hollywood—the producers and studio heads, and sometimes agents and personal managers, frequently use performers without concern for them as individuals and certainly not as artists who may provide the world with rich acting for a lifetime. Actors who are thought to have money in them are sought by all the bosses at the same time. These actors are used in thinly-veiled carbon copies of their previous successful films. They are encouraged to trot out the same mannerisms and qualities in each performance, and when their box office potency wanes, they are trashed. James Coburn, Sandy Dennis, Troy Donahue, and nearly all of the 1980's so-called "brat pack" actors are stars one year and gone the next. Those who would like to be stars must realize that from the point of view of the money men, leading actors in the film industry are not artists but are simply meat to be sold off the butcher's block.

Humphrey Bogart, an actor who did not immediately become a star and fought a long, hard battle to become a "name" performer, talked about the close relationship between box office and stardom: "The words 'movie star' are so misused they have no meaning. Any little pinhead who does one picture is a star. Gable is a star. Cooper is a star. Joan Crawford, as much as I dislike the lady, is a star. But I don't think the so-called others are. To be a star you have to drag your weight into the box office and be recognized wherever you go."

Bogart seems to have understood what some of the elements are that make a star. In describing Gable and Crawford as stars, he suggests that actors playing leading roles who have a touch of sexual swagger to them seem attractive to audiences. Sexual swagger suggests something dangerous, something both desirable and threatening. Certainly this helps explain the mystique that built Bogart, a rather haggard, small-statured actor, into a star. Without the authority, without the veiled sexual swagger, without the confidence, there's no romantic charge to an actor's presence. Interestingly enough, the same sense of authority seems to be true for leading ladies. Those who have significant stage or film presence usually have an ego that shows; you know that they think well of themselves. This cockiness, this self-confidence, is considered unseemly in a woman; it's a quality that is usually described as un-flattering in women. Yet, if one looks at the major women stars in films, especially those who have enjoyed long, successful careers, they all seem to have this quality.

Conversely, there is another kind of actor whose appeal may be ascribed to their "vulnerability." The audience feels that this character is ill equipped to cope with the hard, avaricious, and insensitive people

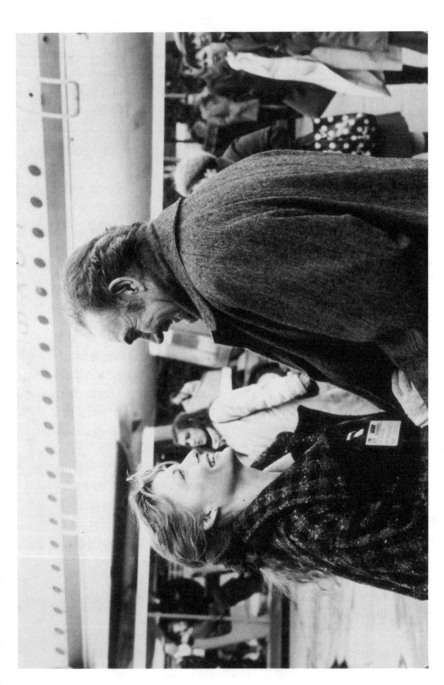

Michelle Pfeiffer and Sean Connery in THE RUSSIA HOUSE

Two actors who personify the kind of "sexual swagger" that can lead to stardom are Michelle Pfeiffer and Sean Connery. Both performers fill the screen with authority regardless of what kind of character they are playing; there is a kind of recklessness in their performances that excites. Both actors have played roles of considerable range, but whatever they play has a kind of life-affirming sexual charge to it that the audience finds arresting.

who abound in this world. The audience experiences two emotions in response to such an actor: first, the audience wants to "protect" the character; there is an element of maternal-paternal feeling in this. Secondly, the audience experiences vicariously with the character, feeling that they, too, are sensitive, vulnerable people pitted against the calloused and unfeeling. Such heroes and heroines are part of our theatrical history from Lillian Gish through Judy Garland to Michelle Pfeiffer. In actors, this vulnerability has been seen in such diverse individuals as Henry Fonda, James Dean, Montgomery Clift, and Marlon Brando. For all his sexual swagger when he was a young actor, Brando epitomized "vulnerability" in his roles in *The Wild One, On the Waterfront,* and *Last Tango in Paris.* Robert Redford, who may not be threatening but certainly has sexual swagger in his film roles, made some interesting observations about playing leading roles. "I don't think critics often appreciate enough what kind of character work can go into leading man roles. They think someone is walking through a part, or just being this or being that. It's very hard to play straight, good people. You can see certain actors who are scared of it . . . any role that I play is approached from character—not from me, my own persona. But I think anybody's own persona is in a film, is in a part. I want to see the person in the character. I'm not really impressed with actors' performances that are purely character. What they completely eliminate is themselves. I can admire the techniques of it, but I'm really not much interested. I want to know who's there along with the character."

Kirk Douglas supports this notion in his book *The Ragman's Son.* He writes, "I had always admired Bruce Dern as an actor. I thought that maybe this would be a movie (*POSSE*) that would make him a big star. It didn't. I realized later that he would always be a character actor because he thought of himself that way. In the scene that opens the picture, he comes out of a barn. Walks out, looks around. The first time he did it, he came out of the barn, looked around and squinted, his face all scrunched up. I said, 'Go back in the barn. Think that you're Gary Cooper and open the door. Walk right out and don't do anything. Just look around.' He looked handsome."

I think Douglas is reiterating what many stars have always known and that is that the personality of the actor must not be lost in the characteri-

James Dean in EAST OF EDEN

Young Henry Fonda, Montgomery Clift, James Dean all share one characteristic: "vulnerability." They seemed so bruised by the vagaries of life that they needed to be shielded from further hurt. What was their appeal? For women these actors fired their deepest maternal feelings, their need to protect. For men these actors seemed to share their sense that they are "victims" of a harsh society that has crushed their hopes and dreams.

zation. Instead the performance must be a synthesis of the actor's own personality along with the character created by the screenwriter. The audience wants the star to play parts of himself all the time. When someone asked Spencer Tracy if he got tired of playing himself, the crusty, long-time star replied, "Who do you want me to play? Humphrey Bogart? I feel its all right to bring your own style to a character." An example of this can be seen in the failure of old Paul Muni films to hold the interest of present day audiences. While personality actors such as Cary Grant continue to have their movies shown lovingly on late night television and in revival movie theaters, Muni's pictures have all but disappeared. Bette Davis gave a very good reason for this being the case. "Paul Muni was a fascinating, exciting, attractive man . . . and it was sad to see him slowly disappear behind his elaborate make-up, his putty noses, his false lips, his beards. One of the few funny things Jack Warner ever said was, 'Why are we paying him so much money when we can't find him?'"

Nonetheless, without losing the personality of the actor, that actor must continually allow the audience to see new facets of his or her personality. Stars know how tenuous their position at the top of the ladder is. Sometimes the actor who loves his stardom and all the pleasures and adulation that goes with it, continues to try to emulate that characterization that won him stardom rather than to continue to really find the appropriate characterizations for subsequent roles. He shouldn't try to play a totally different character, but he should look for different emotional resources within himself to use in playing the character. Some deviation from your established image then is admirable, but too great a change is dangerous; you risk losing that part of the audience that has developed fantasies in relationship to your "image."

Furthermore, often surrounded by sycophants, the star is constantly in danger of losing his sense of perspective. Perhaps no work of art is possible without belief in the audience. The star, distanced from others by his Olympian status, is in constant danger of thinking that he is somehow superior to most people. Akin to the aristocracy of another age, he begins to think he has some kind of "divine right." He must remember what all actors need to remember: he must believe in the audience with a kind of belief that has nothing to do with his publicity or the box office figures associated with his work. He must be thoroughly convinced that only the best he can do is fit to be offered to others.

He, as with all actors, must believe in the audience and believe that an actor's peak efforts just barely make him worthy of his claim to success. As soon as the actor ceases to see himself as part of the audience, when he patronizes or plays down to his audience, or when he panders to what he considers those "jerks" out there, he defeats his claim to be an artist. He becomes the salesman of a commodity and the product he is selling cheaply is his own talent. He betrays himself. This is one of the many pitfalls that not only besets stars but all actors when they are asked to repeat over and over again essentially the same characterization.

There may seem to be some contradiction between these last paragraphs and earlier ones where I suggest that it is important that the actor retain a part of himself in each characterization. An actor must strike a balance in his working methods, a kind of synthesis of all the ideas expressed in this chapter.

When all is said and done, it is foolish to pursue stardom. You will spend your time more wisely simply becoming a fine working actor. There's no logical reason why some talented actors have a difficult time working consistently while others who are not especially good actors become stars. Gary Cooper, who was a merely adequate actor but an exceedingly intelligent man, talked about this. He said of himself, "I'm an average 'Charlie' who became a movie star." He told a fan magazine reporter that glamor was all right, "to ease the pain of disillusionment during the beginning of a career, but it drugs the brain during success." He added, "I don't like to see exaggerated airs and exploding egos in people who are already established . . . No player ever rises to prominence solely on his extraordinary talent. Players are moulded by forces other than themselves. They should remember this . . . and at least twice a week drop down on their knees and thank Providence for elevating them from cow ranches, dime store ribbon counters, and bookkeeping desks!"

A star whose variety of roles has proven that he is truly a fine actor, Jack Lemmon, reinforces Cooper's statement and claims that part of achieving stardom is luck: "You have to do the right thing after they open the door, but someone has to open the door. I had some of those doors open at the right time." That's true for every single actor who attains stardom.

CHAPTER 6

PREPARATION: DOING YOUR HOMEWORK

For theatre-trained actors the lack of adequate rehearsals and pre-paration to play a role in a film or TV show is extremely frustrating. What can you do that will help prepare you for those moments on camera that are preceded by the most cursory of rehearsals?

If you are new to films or television it is likely that your first work will be as a "day" player. You many only get a few pages of script and know little of how your character fits into the telling of the story. If it's one or two day's work, your role is probably some kind of functionary: a receptionist, a taxi driver, a hotel clerk, an airline employee, a fussy housewife who pushes the star away to get at an item for sale at a department store, a harassed police officer; the list can go on endlessly. As an actor you shouldn't use such a role to try to propel your career from "bit" player to stardom. First, you want to be believable in the role without calling undue attention to yourself. To use a bit role to try to call attention to your acting brilliance is likely to be counterproductive; it calls inappropriate attention to yourself in a way that throws off the intention of the scene. The audience becomes too aware of this in-dividual who is not central to the story and such a performance can confuse filmgoers; they may wonder, "Who is this person? Should I be more interested in him or her? Are they likely to be significant to the plot development?" The audience does not consciously ask such questions as they watch the action of the film, but it nonetheless enters into their unconscious thoughts and can lead to their confusion regarding the story. It certainly will not please a director, whose foremost concern is the telling of the story.

THERE ARE NO SMALL ROLES ...

Occasionally a very small role in a film can catapult a performer into better roles. Sally Struthers, who went on to fame in the television series *All in the Family,* had such a role in *Five Easy Pieces.* In that relatively small-budget picture, her role probably constituted three days' work, most of it taking place as a "good time girl" having fun in a bowling alley and a coffee shop; she was just different enough in her performance to suggest an adult sexuality coupled with a childish, early-teen mentality. She never went over the top, and she never deflected our attention from star Jack Nicholson, but she complemented his performance in their scenes together. Giving a performance appropriate to the size of the role and its significance to the storytelling may be very important to both the production and your subsequent acting career.

On the other hand, if you are given a role which incorporates several scenes and requires your being involved in the shooting over a period of several days, it is inexcusable to give a monotonous or static performance. You may claim that such a performance is attributable to cursory rehearsals, but more often it can be attributed to the poor preparation techniques employed by the actor.

In the theatre, this actor's work may have proven satisfactory, but in that environment, the actor had several weeks of rehearsal during which he could experiment and have the helpful questions and observations of a director to guide him in creating the character. Film and television do not offer these opportunities to slowly delve into characterization, so one's preparation before the shoot begins must be more thorough on the part of the actor.

FIND THE SPINE

As soon as you receive the script, you should attempt to determine what is the "spine" of the screenplay. Spine is a familiar term to all stage-trained actors that can be approximated to the backbone of the script. Constantin Stanislavsky, the director of the Moscow Art Theatre and the man most responsible for the codifying of the acting technique that we call the "method," called it the "super objective" and related it to the through line of action. The super objective was the main idea of the final goal of each performance. It can be described as the primary thrust that propels the action of the drama forward from beginning to conclusion. The through line of action is the logical action line running through a role and through the script which you, as an actor, can trace in your mind.

Unfortunately, in many television shows, and to a lesser degree in some movies, the scripts are so poorly structured that they actually don't have a spine to help guide the actor in creating a role. If that happens to be the case, it is the wise actor who recognizes this missing element and works doubly hard to keep the audience from recognizing that the script is empty without either heart or backbone. It's the wise actor, then, who infuses his performance with an invented spine, which in the end serves him as a performer as well as the screenplay.

From the moment you receive the script you should be giving intense thinking to how you will play the character. Basic to any characterization, whether onstage or onscreen, is the need to know what is your character's objective. Although every actor learns this early in acting classes, it should be reiterated: that objective can be defined as what the character wishes, wants, desires; it is the character's goal, aim, intent. All the character's actions within a script germinate from his attempt to achieve his objective. You should be well aware of your character's objective and whether the character's objective changes or is forced to make adaptations during the story. You ask yourself, "What does my character want?" You should be able to say, "My character wants to ..." and complete this sentence with the verb that expresses his desire, aim, or goal.

After you have determined your character's objective in the script, look for those obstacles in each scene that get between you and what you want in the action. Seek confrontation, if that is a necessary part of overcoming the obstacle; this results in conflict and conflict is central to any drama. Moreover, it puts your character into the center of the

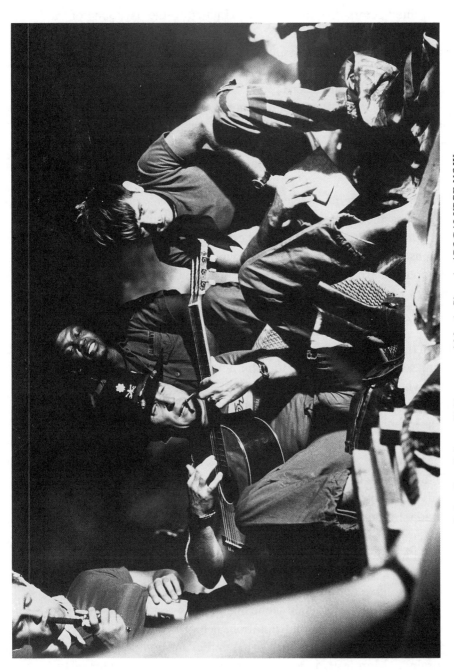

Robert Duvall, Larry Fishbourne, and Martin Sheen in APOCALYPSE NOW
These three characters have experienced an epiphany following a moment of terrible bloodshed in **APOCALYPSE NOW**. Note how the body language and use of rhythm on the part of the actors reveal how different their perceptions of their experience are from each other. Martin Sheen's character reveals in body language that he has learned something that has changed his whole psychological awareness; he has become a different kind of human being.

action. Look for discoveries that you can make onscreen; it's wonderful for an audience when they see a character receiving information that they didn't know before the "here and now" of this moment. Sometimes the actor can enhance a script by making these discoveries in the action, even though the writer may have assumed that the character learned this information in some offscreen action. These "discoveries" may not be revealed in the dialog but can be implied by your reactions, your use of subtext in playing your character, and the subtle changes of body language and vocal response as you learn new information. Perhaps the most exciting discoveries that can be communicated to the audience are those in which your character learns something new about their own psyche that they did not know previously. Skillful actors are always looking for what their character doesn't say but is thinking, feeling, or learning.

DECIDE WHAT'S AT STAKE

Play every scene with something at stake for your character. This can take many forms, but when your character has something at stake you automatically step up the urgency and consequent impact that your character has on the scene. For example, you may wish to win the approval of a superior by your exemplary behavior, or you may wish to make your acting partner see that you are worth loving, or you may want to manipulate your acting partner's character so that they will acquiesce to some career objective that you have that requires their support.

For each scene in the screenplay or teleplay in which you appear, it is important for you to decide what your character was doing prior to this scene. Most of the time nothing in the script will suggest what this action may have been, but you as an actor must provide for yourself this prior action. Suppose you are playing a scene in which you are a shy character who sees a lovely woman in an elevator; you want to meet her but do not know how to get a conversation started. What were you doing in the action that preceded this ride on the elevator?

The scriptwriter has not given you any clues. As the actor playing the role, you might imagine yourself sitting alone at a coffee shop counter in the building that houses the elevator. You were drinking coffee, casually looking through a magazine that includes pictures of attractive and, in your mind, unattainable women. You glanced up from the magazine and your eyes secretly observed happy men and women laughing and enjoying each other's company as they sat in the coffee shop booths. You felt lonely, unattractive, estranged from the people in your age group. Finally, you pushed your coffee cup aside and made your way to the elevator. This scenario that you as an actor invented as the moments that take place before the action of the scene in the script prepares you psychologically; your work in the script's elevator scene is automatically richer.

To avoid your characterization's including irrelevant impulses and unfocused experimentation, you must use your preparation time to find the appropriate physicalization necessary to illuminate the inner life of your character; don't just vaguely think about your characterization in your scenes but put your character into action trying out how he walks, moves, and sits along with the way he talks and uses sounds. The fact that you have conceived the scenes in physicalized and vocalized terms will make your acting stronger. The sounds that you work on at home will help to make your characterization rich and colorful.

By sounds we mean the groans, sighs, moans, chuckles, snorts, throat clearings, and myriad sounds other than words that are natural to humans. While rehearsing by yourself in the confines of your living room, you will find that some of these explorations should be incorporated into your characterization and some of them should be discarded. The important thing is that you are doing these things, many of them on your feet, in preparation for your appearance onscreen and you will not be wasting valuable shooting time making these discoveries on the set.

As I said earlier, I know a director who advises actors to stand in front of a mirror and rehearse their scenes; he says that the actors should evaluate their facial reactions and body movement assessing their effectiveness on camera. This seems to me most harmful advice. Generally, I feel much the same about actors watching the rushes. "Rushes" are those snippets of film recently shot that have come back from the processing lab and are then run for the benefit of the producers, director, and cast that are sometimes shown in the evening following the day's shoot. While I think they are very beneficial for the producers and director, I think that they may be as detrimental as they are helpful to an actor. For the most part I think actors are better off if they never see themselves. It only makes the actors self conscious and fearful, and starts them editing their performance before it is completed. You cannot completely surrender yourself to the character you are playing and congruently assess the effectiveness of your work. An actor who is serving simultaneously as an actor and as his own critic is doomed to fail.

At the moment of creativity, during that moment when you are actually either rehearsing or playing the role, it is impossible to be inside your character and simultaneously evaluate what you are creating. The actor standing in front of the mirror has removed himself from the subjective inner life of the character and, in assessing the character, steps outside of the character and watches himself. In front of the mirror, the actor will make faces, do "schtick," and create the character from the outside rather than from the inside, which will lead to a mannered, self-conscious performance.

Academy Award-winning actress Mary Steenburgen says, "I don't ever practice anything in front of a mirror because I don't want to know what I'm going to do. All I do think about is how I 'feel' about certain things that are going to happen within the scene. But I don't ever plan, ever, the way I'm going to say a line."

Whether the actor sees himself in the rushes or rehearses a scene in front of a mirror, he is not going to like what he sees. Actors, generally, have vulnerable egos; they begin to see their performances as frightful, a piece of fraudulence imposed on the public. Furthermore, they begin to communicate this concern about their performance to fellow actors and to the director, and this is counterproductive. Instead of looking at the rushes or into the mirror, they should trust their inner gut feeling about whether a scene is working or not. That is more dependable.

Steenburgen has other good advice for the actor who is preparing for a film role. "I try to choreograph a part the way you would a piece of music, to know where your highs are and where your lows are, where you come forward and where it's somebody else's moment and you should pull back a little bit. I can almost do it by just reading the whole script over and over and making notes about each scene. If you do a scene just acting your guts out, when you put it together, it's not

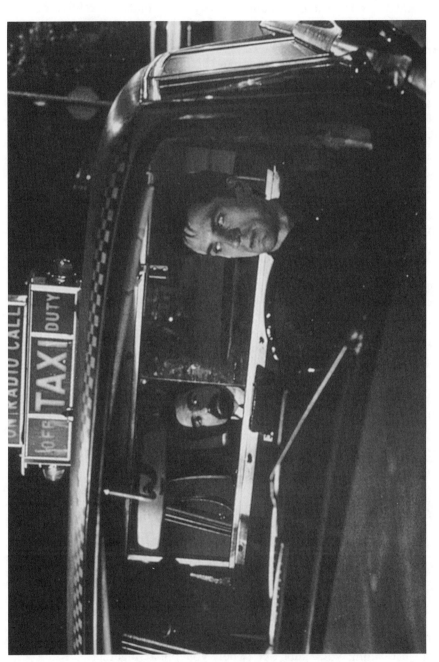

That's director Martin Scorsese doubling as an actor in the back seat, appearing in a telling sequence with Robert DeNiro from TAXI DRIVER. Robert DeNiro has always been perceived as one of film's finest actors, but his work made enormous strides forward in TAXI DRIVER. His acting took on a subtlety not previously seen; he had learned to appreciate the camera's ability to read the inner life of the character if the actor's subtext is sufficiently strong. Note here that his eyes reflect the growing paranoia of the character.

interesting. It's got to have movement and richness and structure and tone to it, the same way a piece of music does."

Some "method-oriented" actors may quarrel with Steenburgen's "choreographing" her performance, claiming that they are artists so they'll just do what they do and not take into account what the camera records. These are method actors who are more interested in the process than the results of their performance. "It doesn't work that way," method actress Steenburgen states. "You can emote like crazy in front of a camera and then do the same thing and do something different with your eyes, and the whole thing is rendered more powerful. I mean, there are a million technical things you can learn about using the camera. And you can say, 'Well, gee, those are tricks. I don't want to learn that.' Well, fine, don't learn it, but your performance will be less powerful than if you learn that film is a marriage between the technical and the artistic. You leave out the artistic and become a purely technical actor, it's going to be boring. If you only do the artistic and don't bother to learn any of the technique, it's boring. You can really use that camera to your advantage. It can be your friend or it can be a foe."

PERSONALIZING THE SCRIPT

You should read the script looking for those ways in which the character and you have similar traits. What hopes, dreams, and concerns do you share with the character you are playing? How can you incorporate "personalization" into the character? By personalization we mean that process by which the actor makes every aspect of the scene vitally alive and meaningful to himself. Personalization is that device in which the actor remembers carefully and concretely an action, person, place, or incident in his own life that can be transferred in part to the experiences of the character you are playing in the film. For example, the actress who whispered, "Last night I dreamed I was at Manderlay" in that old classic Hitchcock movie *Rebecca* could not simply talk about some mythological place but needed to conjure up in her mind some huge, formidable-looking and, ultimately, terrifying place that was so real in her mind that, indeed, she may have actually seen or walked through such a place at some moment in her life.

As much as possible, you need to find analogous visual images taken from your own experiences that are pertinent to the character you are playing. Whatever you do on film is enhanced when somehow you find a way of relating it to your own life. Furthermore, you need not restrict your choices to only those everyday experiences you have had in your life; you can always tap into your fantasy life as well. For example, suppose your role requires you to speak of someone dear to you—a spouse or a lover—who has died. You simply cannot afford to generalize about such a person; you must think of someone you love dearly who may for that matter be alive, but you develop a strong image of that beloved person in your mind and then fantasize how you would feel in the event that person so dear to you died. Developing this ability to personalize the dramatic situation intensifies your sense of immediacy, spontaneity, and skill at making the character's experiences your own.

When an actor's personalization is aided by images as well as words, you will see in your mind's eye a kind of "movie sequence" that is applicable to that which your character is experiencing. More often than not, these vivid images are drawn from your own life, but it gives your performance an extra edge, a more acute sense that your character is truly experiencing what he is supposed to be experiencing at that moment in the script. The more that you can find feelings, ideas, thoughts, and images from your own life experiences that you can use in connection with the words you speak in the screenplay or teleplay—that is, the more you use personalization—the more successful will be your characterization. All of this can be prepared well ahead of the moment that you arrive on the set for the day's shoot.

Obviously, an actor cannot always find in his life approximations to the experiences of the character he must play. In such situations you must apply the "magic if." By this we mean that you make use of your imagination to choose desires and fantasies that you have had which have some similarity to those of the character you are playing, even though the circumstances that triggered those desires and fantasies in yourself may have been entirely different from those of your character.

I think it is very important for the actor not simply to think about the life of his character up to that moment when the action of the character begins in the screenplay, but to follow a formula of questioning about the character that you can apply to each role you do. These questions should be answered in a sentence or two, and I would advise you to write the answers on paper; the actual writing down of these answers is a kind of discipline that forces you to be specific and will help you to avoid the kind of nebulous generalizations that can cause an actor to lose focus and give a poorly defined characterization. Answering these questions inevitably creates a richer, more dimensional character:

1. How old am I? Do my nationality, race, or religion have anything to do with my character's behavior? Do they have anything to do with any specific traits I might have?

2. What is my family background? Are my parents alive or dead? Do I love my parents? Have I favored one parent over the other? Why? Have I any brothers or sisters? How have they affected my life? Am I married? Happily? Are there any children? If not, why?

3. What kind of education have I had? Has it been beneficial? How has it influenced my life?

4. What is my social status? Do I like the people with whom I associate? Do I like the places I go and the things I do? Am I satisfied with my social status?

5. What are my politics? Did I inherit this point of view or arrive at it though other influences? Have my political views changed over a period of time? Why?

6. What are my prejudices?

7. How do I feel about my sex life? Am I happy about it or dissatisfied? Does this affect my behavior in any way?

8. What kind of temperament do I have? What emotions do I express openly most often? What emotions do I try to hide? Why? Am I a highly structured person or easygoing and relaxed? Am I flexible or rigid in my behavior and in my viewpoints? Am I life affirming or life negating? For me is the cup always half full or always half empty?

9. Are my moral standards and my ethical values the result of heredity or environment, or are they a reaction against my heredity and environment? Do my moral standards reflect personal strength or weakness or, simply, the standards of the times and my peer group?

10. What personality peculiarities do I have? Am I generous or selfish? Why? Is my character compulsive in any way?

11. Are there some experiences that my character has had or not had that have deeply affected my life and influenced my behavior in this screenplay?

12. What deep-rooted attitudes about things—in life and therefore in the scenes—does my character have and express? How are these attitudes expressed?

Once you have answered these questions on paper, you will be playing a character with a very specific past that influences your present actions: you will have created the life of the character. In having used whatever information the scriptwriter has provided you and enhanced that with your imagination by enlarging your understanding of your character's psyche and value system, you will undoubtedly be truer to your intuitive responses to each moment in the script. Doing this kind of preparation means that you will come to the set with a fully formed characterization. Even though you may have never met the actors with whom you will be playing a significant scene minutes after your meeting, this preparation helps you to adjust to the locale of the action, the characterizations of the other actors, and the triggers and stimuli that you will receive from the other characters. It is the rare actor who is this thoroughly prepared when they arrive on the set; with such preparation you can confidently enter into the world of film acting.

CHAPTER 7

THE BUSINESS OF BUSINESS

"How can you not love me when I love you so much?" Sounds like the lament of a rejected lover, doesn't it? And that's exactly how an actor feels when he first goes to Hollywood and then is treated indifferently by the people in the movie business. This indifference to a person who has devoted his life to becoming a fine actor results in many a promising performer's returning home from Hollywood a year or so after having gone there to begin a career. The lesson to learn from this is that if you don't understand the business, you're probably not going to make it in the business.

One of the sad experiences that nearly all acting teachers encounter every so often is the return of a dejected young actor after a disheartening time spent pursuing a career in Hollywood. An actor's career is not for the weak; the amount of rejection you will receive in the first few months cannot be imagined. Usually the actor has enjoyed considerable success in his own bailiwick. People have told him he is talented; they have encouraged him, nurtured him, and bolstered his sense of his own worth. However, in Hollywood during those first few months, months that have a way of extending into years, no one seems interested in him. Almost the first question he is asked is, "Have you got any film on you?" When the answer is, "No, but I've done twenty roles in college and community theatre and I've got this press book full of glowing reviews to show you," it is a shock to see how disinterested the people in the business are toward what he considered a pretty strong, well-prepared background.

It's not really that the Hollywood people question your talent; it's that they quickly envision how difficult it will be to get their peers to take a chance on you. It's a courageous talent agent who will take on a client who does not have any film to substantiate his claim that he is a practiced and worthy actor. This is the first of several "chicken and egg" experiences—that is, which came first, the chicken or the egg?—that the actor will encounter in those first few months in Hollywood. If you don't have any film on you to reassure possible employers that you know your craft, then they won't hire you. If you don't get hired, how are you going to get some film on you?

GETTING THAT CARD

Well, let's assume some kind-hearted, brave agent does agree to represent you. Then he or she has the problem of getting casting directors to see you if you don't belong to the union. Well, you can't belong to the union unless you have a job. But you can't get a job without belonging to the Screen Actors' Guild (SAG). Again, here's the old "chicken and egg" dilemma. Which comes first? The SAG card or the job? Producers don't want to hire someone without a SAG card for less than three day's work, which is the kind of job most new actors would get at the start of a career, because they will be fined by the union. It is rumored that some actors have made deals with producers to pay those fines in order to get that coveted SAG card. Other actors have gotten their SAG cards by first finding a way to join AFTRA or Actors' Equity and thus get in through the back door. Finally, it is not generally known, but there is a clause in the Guild contract permitting a producer to hire a newcomer with no penalty if the newcomer has studied for a reasonable length of time at a recognized school or university and can give documented evidence that he has prepared for a professional acting career.

This fact is nearly never mentioned, so that few newcomers know that if they have this kind of strong background they can get into the union and can be used in a film without the producer's being penalized. The union's job is to protect their existing membership; thus they will do whatever they can to deny you membership. Consequently, it may become necessary to take legal action in order to be accepted into the union. Fortunately, you don't need to be liked by the union leadership in order to have a viable career.

MAKING CONTACTS

One of the current phrases popular in the business world, probably no longer in vogue by the time this book is published, is "networking." While the word will probably become dated, its notion that one achieves one's career goals by developing and nurturing contacts and friendships will certainly hold true. This is as true for people in the performing arts as it is true for people in the business world.

Networking, then, is nothing more or less than making contacts and friendships that will help to lead you into the business. The smart actor recognizes that some part of your socializing involves building up the network of people who know you and, in time, care about you and, when afforded an opportunity, will try to help further your career. This networking all takes time, and it has been my observation that a real working career in films takes from three to five years to get underway.

Those students of mine who have gone on to have successful film acting careers all seem to have certain things in common. First, they don't ever accept rejection as a personal thing. They don't allow the almost-continual rejection experienced in the early stages of building a career to overwhelm them and destroy their sense of self-worth. They continue to plug away at their mundane jobs—working as waiters in restaurants, or parking cars, or typing away on a word processor—to pay the bills. But these actors keep their days open for interviews and auditions. On their nights off from these so-called "civilian" jobs, they attend an actors' workshop. This is important to do since it gives them a sense that they are still actors. Moreover, it keeps their instrument tuned so that when that opportunity does come their skills have not grown slack.

Another reason for participating in an actors' workshop is that it is one more method of networking. After the evening's workshop, join the other actors over coffee or a drink. You'll hear at these social sessions about prospective jobs. You'll learn from "working" actors what they went through before they finally got that first professional acting job. One of the surprising things you'll discover is that other actors will tell you about roles you should try to get, provided they are not competing for the same role. They'll go even further and suggest you to a casting director, if they have that kind of influence. This is an example of the rewards that come from networking. Over a period of time, your network will extend to include casting directors, producers, directors, and such diverse people as film crew members who may, indeed, have the ear of someone who can help you enter the business.

If you have the stamina and the perseverance to become an actor, and if you can take the many disappointments that usually prevail in the early years of building a career, you will eventually make your living as an actor. A talented young actor friend recently told me, "I love the pursuit." As soon as he said this I thought, "He'll make it as an actor." An actor who has this attitude must eventually have a career.

STAYING ALIVE WHILE LOOKING GOOD

So you've just gotten off the plane and you're ready to embark on that fabulous acting career. What do you do? First, unless you are independently wealthy, find some kind of work that keeps bread on the table, a roof over your head, attractive clothes on your body, and personal anxiety away from your psyche.

While I can't be of any assistance regarding your psyche, I can recommend that you never minimize the importance of how you dress and how you look. The age of torn levis, sweatshirts, and the "I'm a rebel" look is long gone. James Dean would be in his late middle age now; Marlon Brando is a bit further down the road than that. That kind of look may be acceptable in a university theatre, but it's a turnoff in the motion picture business. Back at the university, you could audition for a role looking like a "poor student" and it didn't matter because most of the directors already knew you through classes and campus social gatherings.

Don't hope to get an agent or interest a casting director by saying, "If they can't judge my talent regardless of my clothes, to hell with them!" That says more about your self-destructive psyche than it ever says about the agents' or casting directors' skills. Come on! You want the job, don't you? Give the casting people every break you can by looking as "right" for the role as you can.

This almost never means you should be wearing a suit with a buttoned-down collar. After all, "suits" is the descriptive name that creative people give to the non-creative people in the business. However, you should always be clean, dress casually yet stylishly, have an attractive hair style, and have a distinctive appearance that separates you from those around you.   No significant actor has ever made it without setting himself or herself apart from the crowd; find the way that you can look unique without being bizarre, full of vitality without being hyperkinetic. In short, be distinctive.

GETTING AN AGENT

Once you have dealt with these hard realities, the next thing you must do is acquire an agent. Don't try to get your own jobs. Making the rounds of interviews and auditions without representation does not impress casting directors and producers. In Hollywood, getting work without an agent is nearly impossible. Furthermore, without representation, an actor often doesn't know about potential acting jobs. It's part of an agent's work always to be aware of forthcoming film and television projects and of the casting opportunities associated with these projects. Casting people are not going to want to see you unless you have representation, so your first objective is to get an agent.

Getting an agent is tough. Most agents are reluctant to take actors without film credits because it's so difficult to convince those who do the hiring to take a chance on a newcomer. Getting an agent is important, but more important is getting the right agent. You will find a list of franchised Screen Actors' Guild agents at the SAG offices at 7065 Sunset Boulevard, Hollywood, CA 90028. Perhaps more helpful is a valuable listing revised monthly called *The Agencies.* What makes it valuable is that it not only provides a listing of the agencies but also provides a fairly accurate assessment of their individual virtues and faults. This can be found at the Samuel French bookstores at 7623 Sunset Boulevard in Hollywood, telephone (213) 876-0570, and at 11963 Ventura Boulevard in Studio City in the San Fernando Valley, telephone (818) 762-0535.

Start your quest for an agent by sending out a glossy 8″ x 10″ photograph of yourself that is an accurate depiction of how you look. Glued or stapled to the back of this photo should be a resume that details your experiences in the performing arts, your education, including drama training, and those skills that you possess that may be significant to a casting director. All of this should be put into a manila envelope large enough to accommodate an 8″ x 10″ photo without folding it along with a brief letter introducing yourself, asking for an interview, and assuring the prospective agent that you will telephone him within a few days. The letter might read like this:

Mr. David Starmaker
Starmaker and Associates
1001 Rodeo Drive
Beverly Hills, CA 90210

Dear Mr. Starmaker:

Look at my picture, and I look like lots of young actors who are seeking representation. Look at my resume with its detailing of productions in which I've acted, awards that I've been given, and the strong training I've received, and I think you will agree I've more to bring to the performing arts than many actors in my age category. Can we talk together about the advantages of working together?

I'll call you within the week and, hopefully, we can see whether it's intelligent for both of us to have me represented by your agency. Thank you.

Very Sincerely,
Kelly Larsen
1020 Wonderland Blvd.
Los Angeles, CA 90068
Tel: (213) 676-3021

Or you might wish to use this sort of letter to introduce yourself:

Ms Lydia Davis
The Friar Agency
9001 Sunset Blvd.
Hollywood, CA 90069

Dear Ms Davis:

Before you take one look at the enclosed photo and hastily throw it into the circular file, please read my enclosed resume. I'm not what you would call a "pretty face," but I think I have a look, and the talent to back it up, that is saleable.

I'll call you within the next few days and, hopefully, you will take a few minutes from your busy schedule to meet me. Your consideration is very much appreciated.

Sincerely,
Buzzy Lacey
15 Hero Court
Los Angeles, CA 90028
Tel: (213) 685-0321

Or you may wish to take a somewhat more conservative approach:

Morris, Gage, and Citron
960 Avenue of the Stars
Century City, CA 90072

Greetings:

I'm new to Hollywood but certainly not new to the business. My enclosed resume reflects some of my work in New York and Chicago; I hope it will whet your interest and result in our meeting together to discuss representation.

Within the next few days I will be calling your office; I look forward to your interviewing me to see whether I might be the kind of actor that would enhance your client roster. Thank you.

Yours truly,
Holly Upstart
784 Corbett Lane
Sherman Oaks, CA 91403
Tel: (818) 907-2816

On the following page is an example of the kind of resume that you should send to prospective agents. Undoubtedly, once you have secured an agent, that person or organization will want you to revise the resume to a format that is consistent with their agency's presentation and a resume that they consider more effective.

BUZZY LACEY

6′ 1″, 175 lbs   AFTRA/AGVA
Brown Hair
Blue Eyes
Age Range: 18 - 26

Film/Television:

Casey, *Twice Damned, Once Blessed*	Comedia 2 Productions
Todd, *A Matter of Conscience*	Tyman-Marvel, Inc.
Tyler, *Simon and Carole*	Continental Playhouse, PBS

Theatre:

Scapino, *Scapino!*	Onstage Repertory Company
Weston, The Fifth of July	TheatreFest
6 roles, *The Dining Room*	Onstage Repertory Company
Leading Player, *Pippin*	Gotham Productions
Ed, *Torch Song Trilogy*	Hale University Theatre
Prince, *Merchant of Venice*	Lark Shakespeare Festival
Phil, *Loose Ends*	TheatreFest
Riff, *West Side Story*	Metro Civic Light Opera
Eugene, *Biloxi Blues*	TheatreFest
Phillipe, *La Ronde*	Hale University Theatre

Education:

BA, Theatre Arts, Garrick College; MFA, Acting, Hale University. Professional training with Stella Adler, William Hickey, Circle in the Square.

Skills:

Snow and water skier, expert horseback rider (English and Western Style), jazz dancer (4 years training), tennis player, swimmer, baritone, can speak with Southern, English, Italian, and German dialects.

Buzzy Lacey
15 Hero Court
Los Angeles. CA 90028
Tel: (213) 685-0321

PHOTOGRAPHS

Before you invest a lot of money in photographs, send your prospective agents a single head shot of you along with the resume. If an agent decides to represent you, he will probably advise you about the kind of pictures to have taken that he believes best represents you and will help grab the interest of casting directors and producers. You will need to put together a composite 8" x 10" glossy that includes at least four shots of you, each one representing a different aspect of you. They should look natural and show you in different kinds of settings that will help trigger various ways that you could be cast in the minds of casting directors. At least one of these pictures should be a head shot and one should be a full-length shot that reveals honestly what your body looks like. (Later in life, when you are a success, you can indulge in airbrushing and other techniques to look younger, slimmer, and whatever fantasies you wish to have about your "image.") At the beginning of your career you must present yourself honestly if you want to get a career going.

If you also want to be considered for commercial work, then you need to get different kinds of photographs for this purpose. Acting in theatrical features and television dramas and comedies is essentially representational, while performing in commercials is essentially presentational and requires quite a different kind of attitude that you bring to the work. If you are not an ingenue or juvenile, but more likely to be cast in leading man, leading woman, or character roles, I think it wise not to do commercials until you've become somewhat established as a film-TV actor. While the money for commercials is very inviting, it identifies you as a certain kind of performer and frequently makes it more difficult to be taken seriously as an actor when being considered for films or television dramas. Conversely, if you are reasonably young and attractive, then you may begin your acting career with commercials without this harming your long-term career objectives.

Before you choose a photographer, check him out as much as possible. Insist on seeing examples of his work. Ask established actors about his work. A good photographer can help your career leap forward; a bad photographer can slow down the process.

At this point before you begin to be interviewed by prospective agents, it is important that you be warned that there are parasites hovering around the edge of the film business that can be harmful to you. Among these charlatans are agents who have not been franchised by the Guild; these nonfranchised agents have virtually no access to casting directors of union films or AFTRA shows. With few exceptions, they are people who prey on the gullible and make their money from such periphery activities as steering you to a certain photographer from whom they receive a kickback. Some of them will recommend that you need "polishing" as an actor and steer you to a certain acting teacher or drama school. Or they may simply say that they need a fee from you to promote you properly. Whatever their scam may be, run, don't walk, to the nearest exit. In short, the only time an actor needs to part with any money for an agent is when the agent has submitted you for a job and you have gotten the job; then the agent rightfully deserves his commission.

FOLLOWING THROUGH

Once you have mailed your introductory letter along with a photograph and resume to prospective agents, it is probable that you will not receive any written response from them. This does not mean that the agents aren't interested in meeting you; what it does say is that very few people in Hollywood write letters and most agents are overworked and understaffed. Simply follow through on your telephone calls and expect no more than twenty percent of the agents you have contacted to grant you an interview.

While at the University of California Los Angeles, a young actor friend won the Jack Nicholson Award as the most promising young professional actor. He appeared in a showcase at the university, which was attended by many industry casting directors, producers, directors, and some agents. The actor remembers, "I was onstage in the showcase for about seven minutes. After the showcase I sent out one hundred resumes along with my 8" x 10" photos and a covering letter. I told the agents that I would be calling them in a few days and would appreciate an opportunity to meet them. About a week after I mailed the pictures and resumes, I made the telephone calls. I was on the phone for five consecutive hours and talked to about two hundred people—usually receptionists and, when luckier, the agents' secretaries.

"Out of the hundred agencies I had contacted, I got through to ten agents who talked to me on the telephone. Of that group of ten agents, four agents wanted to meet me and actually did get around to interviewing me. Of the four agents who interviewed me, two of them told me that they had similar clients on their list and it would be unfair to their present clients to take on an actor who would be 'right' for similar roles.

"This left me with two agencies who offered to represent me. I liked them both but decided to go with one agency for two reasons: first, it was a bicoastal agency with offices in both New York and Los Angeles which means you are being considered for work on both coasts. Secondly, it has what I'd call semi-names on its clients' list. You know, actors who play feature roles on television and in films—no one whose name means you'll go to the picture but recognizable people whom you know when you see them on screen. That means that the agency has produced results for the clients they have and that it must have fairly good 'entree' into the offices of people in the business."

The award-winning young actor went on to talk about his other experiences that resulted from being in the showcase. "The casting directors I met at the showcase were very nice; they were glad to see me and talk to me even though I hadn't yet secured an agent. Some of them even suggested agencies that might be looking for my 'type.'

"Since doing that showcase, I've learned to write down the names of every contact I make, every company that I have sent a letter to, every person who has interviewed me, and I try to write something down about every person I meet that I may want to use as an opening conversational gambit when I see them again. That way I'm not starting from zero because I can talk to them about something related to them. I follow up every meeting with a 'thank-you' note. Some of my friends think this is overdoing it, but what I'm trying to do is establish some kind of relationship with these people who are already successful in the 'industry.'"

While you are being interviewed by a prospective agent, you should be quietly interviewing your potential agent. You need to be sure that the agent is right for you just as much as the agent needs to assess whether you are someone his agency could represent effectively. An agent may realize that you are talented but are competition for another actor who is already signed with the agency; it would be unfair both to you and to his present client to represent two actors who are appropriate for the same roles. For that reason, a good and ethical agent may consider you an excellent prospect but turn you down out of courtesy to his present client.

There are many good agents who specialize in a certain type of actor; it would be a mistake for you to sign with an agency that does not know how to handle the kind of person you are. If you are a young character actor and an agent's client list is mostly filled with young nubile women whose looks are more important than their acting skills, probably that agent isn't for you. If an agency is large with a huge client list, including a number of "names," and the agency has many agents swirling around in a frenzy of packaging and making megadeals, probably that agency is not for you. As a newcomer, you'd just get lost in all that activity.

You need an agent who comes to know who you really are and has some insight into your psychological makeup and the kind of roles in which you would feel comfortable and excel. You need an agent who would put you up for the right kind of roles in which you would satisfy the producers, fit comfortably in the role, and be following a course of action that would lead to a long and productive career.

When an agent takes on a new client, he is required to sign an authorization contract. The contract calls for the agency to represent you for a stated period of time. However, this contract becomes null and void if the agent does not secure work for you within a specified time frame. It's best to keep in mind that an agent doesn't want to keep you under contract if he feels that he cannot make money from representing you. Depending on the stature of the actor, the agent will plan different strategies in approaching potential buyers. If you are a relatively young, unknown actor, then the agent will probably find it necessary to have you meet many casting directors and other individuals who are active in casting films and television roles.

Talent agent Charles Adams Baker, who was with the William Morris Agency for twenty-three years, discussed his relationship to acting clients. "Your obligation as an agent is to get employment for your clients . . . you have to use your experience and discretion to decide what is proper to create and maintain a career." Advising actors, he makes this important point, "You don't want just any job, because the wrong one will kill someone quicker than none at all. In the best sense, an agent really has a sublimated parental role, like a psychiatrist or a clergyman. You're the one father figure in a world of cutthroat commerce."

Once you get an agent, you can't sit back and wait for him to phone you. Every day you must make every effort to keep abreast of what is happening in the business; you should read the trade papers (*Variety, Hollywood Reporter, Drama-Logue*). Quite a lot of the information you read in these publications is published after the fact when casting has been completed, the deal consummated. Nonetheless, you will sometimes get information in the "trades" that can lead to possible work; it's the kind of information that you should share with your agent. It's a way of prodding your agent to get you interviews for projects for which you might be suitable. You have to do a kind of balancing act in which you keep your agent working for you without annoying him so much that he wishes you were no longer his client.

Having secured an agent, you will probably be sent on a number of interviews. Your first interviews will be with casting directors. These interviews in some instances lead to subsequent interviews with producers and, occasionally, a director. In television, the producers make the final decisions about casting; in theatrical films, the director is frequently the final arbiter of who is cast. The interviews may lead to the casting director's asking you to audition for him. If the casting director knows your work, he may forgo an audition but still may ask you to do a "cold reading" for a specific role. Every encounter that may eventually lead to casting is a little different, and the actor must keep flexible and understand that a simple exchange of pleasantries between actor and casting director may actually lead to being cast.

No two interviews are the same, but keep in mind that it is as uncomfortable for the interviewer as it is for you. Make it easy for him. Start by being yourself as much as possible. Actors have a tendency to surround themselves with psychological character armor to protect themselves from what they perceive as a hostile world. Somehow you must forgo the need to wear that mask that covers up your true self.

AUDITIONS

Auditioning may be unpleasant, but it is a necessary part of the business. Assuming that your interview has been a success, then it's quite possible that the casting director will ask you to do a cold reading in which you are partnered with someone on staff or, better, with another actor who is being considered for a role in the same vehicle. He may ask you to audition with a brief one- to three-minute monolog of your own choosing that you should always have prepared just for such occasions. Doing a cold reading is an art in itself, and we will talk about that shortly.

College-trained and drama school-trained actors, when they audition for film and TV, sometimes keep acting as though the same principles that applied at school apply in a professional situation. If you are auditioning in a college theatre or for a regional repertory theatre, you are competing against a set number of actors for a variety of roles that may require you to characterize away from your own persona.

This will not be the case in films; the casting directors have thousands of actors from which to choose, including people who are almost an exact duplicate of the character described in the screenplay. If they want someone ten years older than you with blue eyes, gray hair, and weighing 135 pounds, they will be able to find just such a person in their files. Don't try to become ten years older, blue-eyed, gray-haired, and 135 pounds. More importantly, don't try to assume the psychological makeup of the character if you know that character is quite different from the kinds of emotional resources that are part of your persona. Audition instead so that you put it into their heads that the character they are seeking should be someone that looks and acts just like you (and you are addressing yourself completely to the notion that you are the right person for the role and personalizing everything in your audition reading), and you may very well change their minds about who and what they were looking for in a role.

When Mike Nichols was casting the *The Graduate,* they were looking for a "young Jimmy Stewart" for the role. Then Dustin Hoffman, a very different kind of actor whom no one would ever mistake for a young Jimmy Stewart, auditioned for the role. It changed the producers' and the director's minds about how the role should be played. Hoffman brought his own persona and personalization to the role. Suddenly Mike Nichols had a whole new vision of how the role should be played. The risk-taking involved in casting Hoffman resulted in a brilliant movie and the launching of the career of one of Hollywood's most versatile and brilliant stars.

If the casting director wants you to do an audition monolog that you have prepared for such occasions, it is a cardinal rule that you should stay away from over-familiar material. Absolutely no Tennessee Williams, Arthur Miller, David Mamet, Sam Shepard, or any other dramatist whose work is likely to have been seen and heard by those doing the auditioning. Don't go to those monolog books that are used frequently by acting students; everything in them is known so well by the people auditioning that they can probably mouth the words right along with you.

Try to come up with original material from sources not ordinarily used by actors for auditions. For example, you will find lots of fictional characters who speak for a minute or two in William Goldman's novel *Boys and Girls Together.* This novel is filled with appropriate monolog material and it is almost never used by actors. You will find comparable speeches suitable for monologs in the novels of John Irving, John Updike, and other contemporary novelists. The moment that you choose to use material from these kind of sources, dialog and situations that are unfamiliar to the auditioners, you are already making yourself more interesting to them.

Another reason for choosing unfamiliar material is that the people who are judging you cannot compare your performance to some cele-brated or well-known actor who has done the role before. Comparisons are odious, and who wants to be compared to Marlon Brando or Vanessa Redgrave? If the material is new to the auditioners, they can't question your interpretation based on the work of other actors they've seen before; they can only say that they were excited or not excited by what you have done.

You never know when you may be called upon to do an audition monolog, and last-minute cramming for an audition is likely to produce an awkward, anxiety-ridden, not fully prepared presentation. Have at least one dramatic and one comedic piece ready to be seen. In Hollywood, actors are forced to audition and audition, sometimes several times a week, sometimes repeatedly for the same producers. Never feel put upon by this request, for it is a sign that the casting director thinks well of you and wants someone else who may have final approval of casting see you. This is especially true in television, where network executives, producers, sponsors, and Lord knows who else may have some input into the ultimate casting. Whether you are being watched by one person or many, each time you audition for the same role, give it all you've got. Who knows? It may mean being cast in a television series that plays for years and results in all the principals' becoming millionaires!

Many new actors run into trouble in auditions because they have an incorrect image of themselves and, consequently, choose monologs that are wrong for them. Knowing who you are and the way that others perceive you is an essential part of becoming a successful actor. You need to put your own stamp on your audition monolog and any subsequent cold reading that you do, but first you have to know who you are. It's knowing who they are and choosing to bring those qualities to every character that they play that has made actresses such as Katharine Hepburn, Glenn Close, and Michelle Pfeiffer so good.

FINDING YOUR IMAGE

A friend of mine, an excellent actor, asked, "How, as an actor, does one know what one's image truly is? It's taken me seven years to know me and I'm still not quite one hundred percent aware. How can actors find out their image? Or, rather, the best way to 'sell' themselves?" I don't think I can give a very satisfactory answer, but some thoughts come to mind. Certainly one sells himself best when he is selling what is very true in his own psychological makeup. When Katharine Hepburn was asked to join the ensemble-oriented Group Theatre, she responded "Oh, that's all very well and good but I'm going to be a star!" It was more than ego and ambition; it was simply her recognition that her persona was larger than life, not a team player but a leader or no player at all. She has never attempted to conform to the norm and, in spite of turbulent ups and downs in her checkered career, persisted in remaining her unique self. Over the long run, her image (which once resulted in her being called box office poison by movie exhibitors) has worked for her. She certainly never tried to alter her image so that she would not be box office poison.

In the heyday of the movie business, each studio had its own list of contract players. These were actors whose very appearance on the screen struck an immediate response in the audience. From the moment the actor made his appearance on the screen, the audience knew how they should feel about the character. Actors as disparate as Sydney Greenstreet, Peter Lorre, Helen Broderick, Claire Trevor, Edward Everett Horton, Joan Blondell, Elisha Cook, Jr., Thomas Mitchell, and Marie Windsor all had "images" that provided the audience with a kind of shorthand knowledge of how they should feel about the character. There was, of course, much that was wrong about such "typecasting," but these were all good actors of considerable skill. They knew what was expected of them when they were cast in a part, and they delivered that kind of performance, one that conformed to that image.

Nowadays most stars have images so that we, as an audience, have rather specific expectations about the kind of character they will play and how we should feel about this character: Jack Nicholson represents the masculine iconoclast that isn't afraid to break out of the confines of acceptable social behavior; Clint Eastwood represents the masculine "man of action," a "loner" whose actions speak louder than his words; Sylvester Stallone represents the man who basically distrusts the so-called intellectuals who in his films are portrayed as devious and manipulative. He is motivated by his heart and good intentions rather than by pragmatic thinking.

Jack Lemmon, now that he is no longer young and playing comic roles in such films as *Mister Roberts* and *Some Like it Hot,* has taken to playing Stallone's despised intellectuals. He has become the thinking man, well intentioned, who finds no easy solutions to complex situations. He plays characters who are troubled and uncertain of what course of action to take in contemporary situations where knowing what is "right" and what is "wrong" may be too simplistic and not easy to define. Glenn Close, Jane Fonda, and Meryl Streep are perceived as "feminists," women who usually make choices independent of their mates. Marilyn Monroe, of course, had an "image" of being highly dependent on whatever man figured prominently in her life. All of these stars have images that the audience, regardless of their different kinds of socioeconomic backgrounds, subliminally respond to in similar fashion.

In present day films, the supporting actors are likely not to have such strong images. In some respects this is good for the audience who has to learn how they should feel about a character, but it makes the task of getting established as an actor more difficult. Long before one's professional reputation is established, then, the actor must decide for himself what kind of imprint he wants to make on the audience. Bo Hopkins, a very successful actor who has enjoyed over twenty-five years in films, is a case in point. Although he has never achieved major stardom, he has appeared in above-the-title roles in lesser films and in secondary roles in major films. Sam Peckinpah's *The Wild Bunch* was his first breakthrough in the business, and his vivid portrayal of a bright-but-crazy youth, reckless but lovable, a kind of young "good ol' boy" has been his stock in trade ever since. Hopkins is actually quite a sophisticated man who happens to hail from the deep South and has taken advantage of his Southern accent (more pronounced in films than in life) to carve out a niche for himself in the business.

Successful actors seem to invent themselves; they find an image that the audience enthusiastically embraces. I rather doubt that Clint Eastwood, such an intelligent and aesthetically fine director, is actually the same person that his film image projects. Probably Jack Nicholson's image became set with his success as the renegade lawyer in *Easy Rider.* In variations it has continued in *Five Easy Pieces, The Last Detail, Chinatown* and every film he has made since. For most actors their image crystalizes with their first major roles and they are wise to sustain these qualities and expand on those qualities in the work they do thereafter.

AUDITION AND PERFORMANCE

Actors should treat all auditions as a high-level interview. We need to understand that commerce must take place before art takes place and the commerce part is getting the job. Once you get the job, then it is possible to make the art. What should your audition reveal to your prospective employer? It should be an indication of your resourcefulness, imagination, adaptability, and authoritativeness as an actor. You should, in the audition, emphasize those qualities by purposefully attacking the beginnings of lines, revealing vocal colors, stressing personal pronouns (what's more important than the word *me*?), making eye contact with the actors with whom you are auditioning, and finding ways of physicalizing within your environment that suggests your body is comfortable and expressive in performance.

When you finish an audition monolog, really give it a finish. Think of the scene as though it were on film and the scene ended on a slow fade following your dialog. Hold the moment, stay in character, stay inside the character's experience as though you are waiting for the curtain to fall or the scene to fade out totally before the next scene in the film begins. There is nothing so jarring and infuriating for the watcher as having the actor bounce out of what their character is experiencing the second their dialog is finished.

Treat an audition as a thing unto itself: a special one to three minute sequence that must stand on its own as a representation of your work. Make sure you keep this monolog brief; the people auditioning you will know what they need to know within the first ninety seconds. You will not be able to show the casting people your complete range of emotions and technique. Nor should you want to. Keep the audition simple, honest, clean. Always use good energy. Not being able to hear you will scare the hell out of any casting person. The actor who cannot be heard easily in an audition nine times out of ten will not be heard easily when performing, and this can be a liability even on camera with the most sophisticated sound equipment.

If the casting director gives you a scene to read from the screenplay or teleplay, it is probable that he will also give you some time to read over the scene and come to some kind of conclusion on how to play it. If you are lucky, you will be able to do this cold reading opposite another actor who is being considered for another role in the film. If you are doing a cold reading with another actor, look at the other actor as much as possible. Hold the script so that you can obtain eye contact with the other actor whenever possible. Remember that your reactions to the other actor's characterization are at least as important as your line readings. Use the other actor's characterization in the cold reading to trigger some of the choices you make in yours.

Make sure that your cold reading incorporates appropriate physical action as well as line interpretation. You are auditioning for the "movies"; movies move and so should you. It is likely that you will do this cold reading in an unlikely environment. More often than not it will be in a cramped casting director's office with minimum space available, but use that space as imaginatively as you can. If, for example, the script suggests that you might forcefully strike another character, naturally you can't hit that person during a cold reading, but you can make a slight swing with your hand which reveals to those assessing you that you sense what the scene should be if you were actually playing before the camera.

Frequently you will do cold readings with someone who is not an actor (a secretary, a production assistant) and this person, usually unconsciously, assumes a neutral attitude: they work very hard not to act out of embarrassment at their perceived inadequacies. You must play against them as though they are really an actor who is making a good emotional commitment to the moment. If you are not fortunate and the person reading the scene with you is not an actor, it will make your task in doing a good cold reading more difficult. Still, you can reveal your ability to communicate and to listen. Find a way of reaching through to your acting partner regardless of their lack of skill; don't ignore your acting partner because you're not getting enough from him or her. If your acting partner is not a trained actor, he will probably run through the material much too quickly; don't let him set the rhythm of the reading. By your reading of your dialog control that element of the audition.

Sometimes it is the casting director who plays opposite you in the cold reading. When this is the case never touch the casting director; it sets up a symbiotic relationship with that person that may unconsciously trouble them. If you are reading with the casting director, make eye contact with that person as much as possible. Never bury your head in the script.

Even though the time before you start the cold reading is brief, try to get a clear idea of what your character's intentions are in the scene. If you are not sure, still make a choice. Even though it may be a wrong choice, it will give you a specificity in the scene that will reveal to the auditors that you are a thinking actor who can work with authority.

When auditioning, go for broke; give them a full-blown, all-out performance. You may make wrong choices, but that doesn't matter since these choices can be altered once you've been given the role, and casting people, producers, and directors know this. What they want to see in you is risk taking, excitement, lots of energy, and a full emotional commitment, even if you're not quite sure who the character is supposed to be. It is more important at an audition to show the extent of your emotional equipment as an actor than to illustrate your understanding of the script.

Smart casting directors, producers, and directors get interested when they see an actor taking risks—most of them like an actor who goes for the big moment, who gives an audition that takes chances, that is something out of the ordinary. It mustn't become bizarre but it can be unusual. They should be able to look at this audition and say, "Well, it's unusual but it could happen! And the actor is interesting."

When you go to an audition, stop worrying about doing the scene right. After all, how much do you know about the script beyond this particular scene? Are you privy to the director's concept? Have you and the writer discussed the spine of the script? If the answer is "no," and it's likely to be "no," then what you want to do in the audition is to let the people watching you learn who you are. Worry less about the material and more about how you would deal with the situation (as you understand it from the script segment you have seen) as if you were actually experiencing it. Put yourself into the script, not some hastily conceived character foreign to your own experiences.

Don't waste time trying to figure out what the people auditioning you want. Find within the script that which is true of yourself. Trust your own gut-level responses to the material and then work with specific clear-cut intentions. If you have made wrong choices, you have at least shown them that you are an actor of courage and commitment.

Look for the humor that may be in the script. The pressures of auditioning often send humor flying out the window. If it can be justified, find places to laugh, chuckle, be amused. Better still, find a way of putting a spin on the dialog that results in the auditors laughing, chuck-ling, being amused.

Although auditions are frequently given in cramped quarters, feel free to get up and move around if you want. Be careful, though, that you don't get caught in aimless pacing. Also confine your movement to that which would be natural in such a small space. Your movement should be motivated and grow out of an impelling need.

Some very talented actors are lousy at auditions at first. They just don't find it easy to give a good first reading. While all my sympathy goes out to them, I can only say that you've either got to learn somehow to give good cold readings or you aren't going to have a career. Do whatever is necessary to become a good cold reader. If it means reading out loud for one hour daily for six months, do it! If it means taking a speed-reading course, take it! If it means getting someone to work with you for hour after hour until you develop proficiency at cold reading, find that someone! No one is going to listen to your explanation, "I'm really good! I'm just a lousy reader." The casting director's job is at stake whenever they make a wrong choice and they are certainly not going to take a chance on someone who reads badly.

Both in performances and in auditions and interviews, you must always be "up." No one needs the burden of your personal problems. No one wants to know that you've had a bad day. Put the problems of your everyday life behind you when you go on an interview or when you are auditioning. Be positive, life affirming, a confident, well-adjusted individual. You may have to "act" these qualities, but it will make a difference in whether you get the job or not.

Lots of conscientious actors who are really talented make the error of discussing the "problems" of a character or script with the persons who may cast them. Don't make this mistake. What if your casting director or producer or director is insecure? They hear you discussing your concern over some of the complications of the character, some of the challenges of the character, and sometimes they misinterpret this as an uncertainty, a lack of confidence on your part. They read your actor's interest in the challenges of the role as insecurity on your part, and that flames their insecurity. Save that kind of discussion for acting classes and workshop sessions; there they are understood and appreciated.

BEING LIKEABLE

As a former member of the Actors' Studio in New York, I hesitate to say this but, nonetheless, I think it unwise to advertise that you are a "method" actor. Method, in some film circles, has become a bad word since it sometimes connotes an intractable, inflexible, pig-headed actor who is wildly self-indulgent. This may be unfair inasmuch as a good method actor is also a disciplined actor but, nevertheless, discussing one's working methods as an actor may be counterproductive.

People who cast shows know that they are always ahead of the game if they cast people who are likeable. First, it's more pleasant for your fellow actors and for the production people if you are likeable. Secondly, an audience can usually sense when an actor is a likeable person. There are unlikeable performers who have had long successful careers, but in their cases they had to have some fascinating qualities and uniqueness of personality to make up for their disagreeable qualities. There are even actors whom everyone recognizes as having talent, who sometimes garner excellent critical notices, but they still don't succeed because audiences just don't like them. Usually, if the audience doesn't like such an actor there's good cause; the audience senses that the actor is not a likeable person.

If you feel that the first impressions you give people are not likeable and that people do not respond positively to you, it's worth taking the time and expense to try to find out why this is the case. More often than not, the best thing to do is to hie yourself to a psychologist. Together the two of you can explore your past and learn what caused you to have the kind of emotional blocks that cause you to seem to be unlikeable. Conversely, there are many likeable actors who do not know they are likeable and who do not have the freedom to let these positive qualities in their personality show; they, too, will benefit from therapy.

When you go on interviews and auditions, let everyone feel that you would be enjoyable to have on the set. After all, acting is great fun! Communicate to these prospective employers that you are great fun when you are doing what you love. Somehow you must communicate to them that audiences will enjoy watching you even if you are playing a villain or a life-negating person. This may seem contradictory but it isn't. Think of characters such as those that Sydney Greenstreet and Peter Lorre played in those Warner Brothers pictures that usually starred Humphrey Bogart. They played dastardly people, and Lorre often also played a "downer" who had nothing good to say about mankind. But these actors were never downers to watch. Behind their characterizations was an obvious joy in being villainous or playing a downer.

Something of the same kind of joy at playing characters who are people down on their luck, real losers, was communicated in the acting of Dustin Hoffman and Jon Voight in *Midnight Cowboy*. It's a love of acting that is communicated congruently with the truthful performances these actors are giving. The audience loves these actors for the dual messages they are sending in their work. By the same token, when you are being considered for a role, you must communicate the joy that you would bring to the set regardless of what kind of character you are playing.

Always audition for everything you can regardless of whether you think you are right or wrong for the role. How do you know what the casting director, producer, and director are looking for? Don't typecast yourself and narrow the kinds of roles you deem appropriate for yourself. There is something of a paradox here, because I've previously said that it's necessary to know the image that you project to audiences. Unfortunately, sometimes an actor gets caught up in a series of roles that may not necessarily be his true image; they may be roles that a few casting directors saw as appropriate for him and that's how he got his career launched. Now, because casting people sometimes have tunnel vision, this is the way he's always being cast.

Perhaps the casting people never got a true sense of his psychological makeup and the kind of personality he actually has. Perhaps those casting people saw the actor play only certain roles in films and TV and assumed that these roles were the extent of the actor's range. For example, in England an actor who is of East Indian heritage is going to automatically be relegated to roles in which the actor plays store keepers, government bureaucrats, possibly doctors, or other professionals who serve the public; such an actor is always going to be cast as a functionary and never as a sexually interesting person, or a heroic type, or someone for whom the audience should be rooting. It is for such reasons that Merle Oberon carefully kept her East Indian origins a secret. It may be a kind of racism but, more pragmatically, it's just that such an actor has great difficulty overcoming a centuries-old notion of what constitutes being English.

Casting directors in the United States tend automatically to feel the same way when casting Chinese and Japanese actors; it's not that they are prejudiced but they fear that American audiences will not respond to actors who don't quite fit the traditional image of an American. John Lone, the star of *The Last Emperor,* is both handsome and marvelously talented, but his career has been thwarted in part because he's Chinese and it's difficult for casting people to envision him in many roles; the casting people fear that the audience will not be able to get beyond his racial makeup to see the kind of universal human being he is. Nonetheless, actors such as Lone should be put up for nontraditional casting. Perhaps the auditioners think they are looking for a certain kind of person for a role when suddenly they discover you are someone who is exciting and interesting and who has a special "spark" that suddenly changes their mind about who is right for the part. Who knows, they may decide that "you might just work" in that particular role.

CASTING

It's an irony that actors are constantly complaining about type casting but then exclude themselves from auditioning for many roles that they might do very well. It drives directors and producers crazy when an actor decides for himself that he's not right for a role. Too many actors have a very dim notion of what their real skills are and what kind of roles are right for them. If someone wants you to audition for a part, go for it! They must have some valid reason for wanting to consider you for the role. More often than not actors have a rather distorted notion of their own image.

Make no mistake, it helps to have friends in the "industry" who want to see you succeed. That's why it takes a career so long to get launched. It takes several years to build the friendships and contacts so that someone will say, "Yes . . . take a chance on him." Many times you may audition for the same people and be rejected over and over again. Keep coming back whenever you get the chance to audition for them. Sooner or later someone will say, "He's a good guy and he's auditioned a number of times for us and each time he's looked pretty good. Let's take a chance on him!"

When you don't get cast it's devastating. Go ahead and mourn your loss of that wonderful role. Mourn it and then forget it. Too many actors have a very difficult time handling the rejection and this, more than anything else, causes some very talented people to drop out of the profession. Kirk Douglas, in his autobiography, *The Ragman's Son,* writes about the pain of rejection: "That is the pathetic side of our profession, the rejection. They're so shattering, so devastating. The hurt of it never leaves you. The pain is always there: those moments when you think you've got the part; the constant calling back, the false reassurance that you'll get it. Then you don't. It's so humiliating. I discouraged all four of my sons from ever going into this profession. Obviously, they didn't listen to me. But my feeling is, there's only one way to go into this profession, and that is, there's nothing else you can do; you have to do it. The best thing an actor can do is try to stop others from becoming actors. You have to overcome almost insurmountable obstacles to achieve success . . . Rejection is just something that you endure. It doesn't leave you even if you become a star. Then you get rejected on a different level. There's a part that you want to do and some other star gets it. The definition of an actor—someone who loves rejection."

As difficult as it is to do, try to see the casting choices made from the perspective of the producers and directors. You may have been very good in your audition; you may have been the most impressive person the auditioners saw. Well, then, why didn't you get cast? There are myriad reasons that have little or nothing to do with your acting skills. Perhaps the leading man is short statured so the balance of the cast must be on the short side. Perhaps you have too strong a personality for the roles open in the show; you might, in the minds of the auditioners, overshadow the star. More often than not it is that the producers and directors are trying to assemble a cast in which the chemistry between performers is right and, good as they know you to be, you just don't quite fit into that chemistry. When you don't get cast, don't try to analyze the reasons why. There are in all casting situations too many factors, usually unknown to the actor, that play a part in the casting process; to try to guess the reasons why you are bypassed in casting is a futile gesture. It is only after you have auditioned for twenty-five different roles and continually been rejected that you should ask yourself questions.

Even though you may not have been cast in a show, keep your contact with casting people alive. It never hurts to drop a "thank you" note to those who have seen you. If you've got new photographs, slip one into an envelope and send it along to them. If you're doing something on television, in a film, or on a tiny Equity-waiver stage, let the casting people know. To some extent, casting is based on friendships. It makes good sense that a person in a position to cast is going to cast someone they know (and have come to like) if that person is equally qualified for the role. It's human nature to go with the person you know. That's why it usually takes several years to launch a viable acting career. An important part of the business is developing contacts and friendships. There is no Machiavellian plot involved. Wouldn't you, given two equally talented and "right for the role" actors, go with the actor you know? Therefore, become the actor they know.

CHAPTER 8

MERCHANDISING YOUR TALENT

From the Hollywood perspective talent is a product. If it's saleable and a hot commodity on the market, everyone will scurry to get the attention of that product. Sadly, however, today's hottest item can quickly become dated and no longer marketable. Actors need to be aware of this reality and take measures to avoid having their careers cut short by their naivete about the business. When you first achieve success, it is easy to assume that your special qualities as an actor have finally been discovered and it's easy to overlook that even fine actors can be quickly forgotten once the vogue of their "newness" is over. Once a career has been put into motion, it becomes a never-ending battle to keep that career moving. Some of this is partly true of other professions but it is a never-ending reality for actors.

The need for the actor to keep people in the industry aware of the performer was made clear to me when I saw a memorable commercial on television that I thought was extremely well made. One of the pivotal characters in the commercial played a venal politician with special glee. It was quite surprising to me to learn a little later on that the actor I liked was an old friend whose work as an actor was well known to me. I didn't think as I was watching the commercial, "Oh, I know that guy." I didn't even know it was Charles Martinet, even though we've known each other for ten years.

When I related this to Martinet the next time we had lunch together, he replied, "that shows the importance of marketing yourself, because producers see hundreds of actors every day, they see hundreds of television spots in a year. If a friend doesn't know that I was in that commercial, how can these people who see hundreds of other actors know? I have to tell them. I have to reinforce that I was in that commercial and then they can remember, 'Ah, that was a good spot!' And that can lead to more work for me. All that marketing really does is slightly open up more possibilities. It's not going to get you work; it's just going to get you more possibilities of work."

Martinet stresses that high visibility is important for an actor; you've got to constantly remind people that you are a product they should use. Martinet is unknown in Hollywood, but he has a high profile in the San Francisco Bay Area, which is the sixth largest market in the United States. In this secondary market, he is an actor who works with a number of regional Equity theatres, appears almost monthly in commercials, industrials, and the occasional TV theatrical film. "I regularly send out a newsletter detailing the latest happenings in the career of Charles Martinet. I try to couch it in humorous terms since I want the producers and agents to read beyond the first sentence. In addition, I try to be where any events are being held where my potential employers are likely to be. Awards shows are a must, of course. I try to be at every significant benefit show and, whenever possible, participate in them if I can. I attend every social function where the producers are likely to be. I don't think you can go with the attitude 'Oh, I'm going to find a producer and give him my business card.' Seeing them, however, is a way of reminding them that you are part of the 'working actor' community. I think it's important to be in the environment in which the people in your business are converging. It gives them one more chance to recognize that you are a part of the same business as them."

BECOMING VISIBLE

Hollywood actor Ken Letner, a series regular for a season on *Falcon's Crest* and a frequent guest star on such shows as *L.A. Law* and *Designing Women,* shares Martinet's view of the business. "I think I'm more aware than the average actor of the marketing side of the profession.

Whenever I've sent out a resume, whether it was to an agent in the days when I was changing agents or to a casting director, I always wrote an accompanying note saying, 'Dear' and in the blank spot I would always use their first name; I always pretended to know them. Pretending to know them has definitely led to my getting a few jobs. My feeling is that if using first names and appearing to know the person I'm writing leads to one job, then the process has been worth it."

Letner had been a prominent director-teacher in El Paso, Texas, before he moved to Los Angeles. "When I came to Hollywood, I already was a member of Equity but not of SAG or AFTRA. The first thing I did was get a list of the agents, and I sent out a picture and a resume to every single agent and I didn't get one answer! Fortunately I had discovered an actor in El Paso who later became a Hollywood agent, so I went to her for help. She let me use her files and I sent out pictures and resumes to all the casting directors from her office. That action began to get some interest in me. The lesson to be learned from all this is that you have to hustle your own work."

Some of the ways that Letner has hustled his own work are tried and true methods. Actors tend to not follow through on such efforts because it's hard and boring work and because they rarely see immediate results from such efforts. "At an earlier time in my career I always sent out some sort of flyers to casting directors every three or four months," Letner said. "It was usually a mail-out that had some review quotes from my latest play, and I'd always do something in handwriting on the flyer because it's more personal. In my last mail-out I scrawled in my own handwriting that I was guest starring on *L.A. Law*. You send this to everyone you can possibly think of that might help lead you to your next job. In earlier times before jobs came frequently, I would send out cards with my picture up in the corner, a listing of some of my important credits on the card, and then I'd write a personal message in addition to the printed material saying something like 'I know you're working on such and such a project at this time—please think of me.' You always have printed at the bottom of your mailers the name of your agent, his or her address, and their telephone number. I've always put this information into the envelope in such a way so that the first thing they see when they open the letter is what I have written personally.

"Even though at the time I usually didn't know the person I was writing, I always wrote 'Dear Pamela or Bob' or whatever their first name might be. I just sent out such letters to every casting director listed even though I had no expectations of meeting them for any specific reason; this was simply so that if anything came up that I was right for, they would think of me and call my agent. It absolutely works! I recognized that if I got one day's work out of this, it paid all the costs of the printings and mailing and I could still pocket a couple of hundred dollars, so it was always worth it. On each of these mailings, I was writing between two hundred and two hundred and fifty casting directors and in each letter I would include that brief personal note along with the printed material. Even though most of these casting directors had never met me, the note and the whole way I put together the mailing was intended to suggest that somehow we had met and that I knew them. If I didn't have any new reviews to quote, then I'd just say 'Hi! I just wanted to remind you that I'm around,' something direct and something that didn't take them a long time to read. The personal salutation leads the secretary to assume that somehow I know this casting director and the secretary would make sure it gets to the casting director's desk. I also buy ads in the trades (*Variety, Hollywood Reporter*) when I have something prominent that I'm doing; I've gone all the way from an eighth of a page to three-quarters of a page."

DILIGENCE PAYS OFF

Letner continued, "Once I'd sent out my pictures and resume, I'd start knocking on doors and hoping to make human contact with some of these people I've written. Everyone in Hollywood says 'don't do that' but I did. Furthermore, I got an agent who allowed me to have a card that got me on the studio lots, presumably because I was making deliveries. Once on the lot, I just knocked on doors and introduced myself. It took a hell of a lot of courage. You risk, of course, their telling you to get lost. It's like the Fuller Brush sales; you're going to have doors slammed in your face, sometimes you can't pass the secretary, but the risk is worth it. Even if I only got to see the secretary, I'd immediately send a note to the producer or casting director or whoever's office I'd visited saying that I met his/her secretary the other day and she said that I might get an interview with you even if she hadn't said it. She probably wouldn't remember anyway since she comes in contact with so many people."

For all his "salesmanship" in pursuing a career, Letner feels that he has not fulfilled one facet of career building that he considers important. "I think that a young actor in town should try to be as social as you can get. It's the part of the business that I'm not good at doing. When an actor can afford to do so, and especially if they are doing something that is being seen right then on TV or in a film, they should go to the fashionable 'in' restaurants where they'll be seen. When I was being seen weekly on *Falcon's Crest,* I should have been seen in the posh restaurants where producers and directors who frequent these kind of places would see you there and, consequently, see you as one of them, one of their crowd. I think I was wrong to not pursue that aspect of the business more. It's difficult for me to be a party-goer type of person, to deal with the chitchat of that kind of social activity, but I think it's important as part of the selling of your career.

"I believe that I'm in the top twenty percent of those actors who work a lot, and it's my hustle and the fact that I'm out there with all that public relations stuff that's done it. I know that when I'm hustling like that, my agent gets more calls for me than I get when I'm not hustling."

Letner describes a recent time when he was asked to do a "day" part—one day's work—rather than his now usual "guest star" role. He told the casting people he would be willing to do the smaller role, but that he must work at his traditional day's salary which is $1,000.00.

The casting people found this acceptable. To people outside the industry, and certainly to the acting student struggling along on limited funds, this seems an astronomical salary, and it is approximately the same salary that a featured actor on a soap opera receives per day. What people who are not actors fail to realize is that the time it takes for an actor to sell himself in the business is many, many more hours than the acting job itself, so that seemingly astronomical salary must be balanced against the enormous amount of hours of concerted effort it takes to get the job. The problem for many actors new to the profession is their failure to realize that three quarters of their effort is getting the job.

"Talent is a common denominator," according to Letner. "It is assumed that all the working actors are reasonably talented. I don't think I am more talented than the next guy, but in the talent pool in which I compete I am about equal with everyone else. What makes me different is 'hustle.'"

BEING SEEN

One of the ways in which an actor new to Hollywood can begin to be seen by casting directors and producers is to appear in a theater production or talent showcase. These productions are usually staged in tiny theatres seating 99 people or under, often in storefront playhouses which are fairly primitive. Professional actors in Hollywood have mixed feelings about appearing under these circumstances. James DePaiva thinks doing plays in Los Angeles does not help build a career; Letner feels they are beneficial.

"Most of my early work came through two sources: doing theater productions in small theaters and scene workshops that were only open to people in the industry," Letner recalls. "Nowadays you pay a fee to be seen in these showcases by one casting director at a time."

DePaiva says, "as far as doing plays in Los Angeles, you are doing them for your own growth and satisfaction and nothing else. Casting directors do not go to plays in Los Angeles. That became evident to me when my wife, who is a well-known actress, did a play there. When it comes to the smaller venues, people do not go to plays in Los Angeles. The casting directors are a disgrace in a lot of ways. They will have you pay $50.00 to do a scene in front of them, but they won't go to a play that has been rehearsed for eight weeks and played three months. They'd rather go to a dinner party at a posh restaurant."

The way in which showcases operate changes from year to year so that anything we say here is likely to be dated by the time this book is published. You must somehow be sufficiently enterprising to find out what current mode of operation exists when you are seeking showcases. For actors who are searching for showcases, the best source of information about Equity-waiver productions, non-union theatre productions, non-union film casting, and appearing in student films can be found in the weekly trade publication *Drama-Logue,* which can be found at many Los Angeles newsstands. Actors shouldn't scoff at appearing in non-union films; an effective performance in one of these low-budget productions can provide you with some film footage of your work that you can show to producers and casting people. You'd be surprised how many successful actors began their careers in these marginal enterprises.

Depressing, isn't it? All this talk about the selling of yourself as a product. You never hear about it in the classroom, and yet it is an important part of an actor's understanding if he should choose to pursue a career. This may be the first textbook connected to some aspect of acting that addresses the matter. Instead of despairing at the way commerce seems to trample art, think strongly about this merchandising of one's talent. If you can accept the harsh reality that the actor must deal both with the commerce and the art as part of building a strong professional career, then you are several steps closer to achieving your goals.

CHAPTER 9

LIGHTS! CAMERA! ACTION!

SCENES FOR THE CAMERA

The series of screenplays included in this section of *Acting for Films and TV* were selected because they could all be shot on a college campus. While they include a variety of roles that cover a reasonably large range of ages and character types, nearly all the roles can be played by college students.

William Goldman's *Boys and Girls Together* scenes are taken from his novel, while Arthur Laurent's *A Clearing in the Woods* scenes are from one of his early plays. Both works have been edited into film scripts, but no dialog has been altered in any of these scenes. All the other scripts are original screenplays that have not been produced. This choice of unknown material has been intentional since it is better for the actors to be creating roles for themselves, independent of the influence of a well-known actor who may have preceded them in a produced film.

All of these scenes, even though they could be part of a television series or movie, are intended to be shot with one camera. In general, the only kind of filming that employs more than one camera is the television situation comedy shot in front of an audience on the soundstage. These comedies depend upon the reaction of an audience to give them the spontanaiety necessary to their genre. They are shot in the same three-camera style that was born in the age of live television. *Cheers, The Golden Girls,* and the long-running *All in the Family* all use the three-camera shooting style.

Daytime dramas employ three cameras in their shooting as a matter of expediency, since they require nearly four hours of performances a week. The director edits the show as it plays in front of the three cameras. He watches three monitors from the control booth and selects the shots that are shown on the air. Three camera shooting, then, is a kind of compromise filming technique dictated either by the need for an audience or economic and time considerations.

Directors, almost without exception, prefer shooting with one camera. While their control is somewhat restricted by the editor's choices when the film is cut, the influence on the editor is limited to that which he or she can edit. Shooting with one camera helps limit the editor's choices. Furthermore, a good director not only wishes to make each frame of the film visually interesting, which requires shooting with one camera, but wants to control the psychological response of the audience to each moment of the film. This can only be done if the director controls the composition of each image throughout the film.

The highly respected George Stevens was said to shoot every scene in a film from every possible perspective, and he had a reputation for making many "takes" of each scene. It was thought that he did this because he was a careful craftsman, but I suspect it reveals a lack of trust in his own esthetic judgement coupled with an uncertainty as to what he wanted each scene to say to an audience. He covered this uncertainty by shooting the same sequence from several angles, even after many takes of the same sequence. With all these options open to him, Stevens was able to construct the film while editing it, putting the movie together in post production. I've always felt that this approach to filming nearly always resulted in movies that generated little heat, spontanaiety, or intrinsic energy.

Alfred Hitchcock, the master of suspense, went about the business quite differently. Well before the shooting of a film began, he had a clear picture of exactly what he wanted the audience to see in each frame of the film. The composition, lighting, psychological statement of each image, and the esthetic look of each shot was carefully pre-planned and followed meticulously. (Martin Scorsese is an example of a present-day director who maintains the same level of control over a film.)

This approach to filmmaking served Hitchcock well until almost the end of his career. Hitchcock gave his editors few options; each sequence had only one camera setup and there were a minimum number of takes made for these scenes. The final film product in Hitchcock's movies respresented his concept, vision, and esthetic sense, and the editor's influence on the final print was minimal.

Throughout the screenplays, I have interpolated possible choices in camera setups to assist the director/teacher and actors when they are shooting the scenes. In a few instances, I have even discussed possible characterization choices that might be beneficial to the interpreters. These are, however, suggestions only and the director/teacher should feel free to make other choices. Continual experience with the camera will develop the director/teacher's proficiency, and no one should be intimidated by the technical aspects of filmmaking.

Since some of the scenes are several pages long, it may be advantageous to divide the longer scenes into two sections, with one group of actors playing the first half of the scene and another group playing the second half. Moreover, since the most time-consuming aspect of filming is changing from one camera setup to another, it is suggested that the director/teacher have four actors play each role. The use of four teams of actors makes it possible for eight actors to appear on camera in the same sequence, which is an efficient learning experience for the performers.

Do not tell the actors who their acting partners will be until the time of the shoot. Why do I make this suggestion? In motion pictures and television, more often than not the actors will meet for the first time an hour or two before the scene is shot; whatever rehearsal they get will be done within that same hour in which the scene is shot. Certainly, it is rare when actors are given the opportunity to rehearse together in the same way that they would if they were appearing in a play or preparing a scene for an acting workshop.

Actors meet on the set and generally run through the scene once with the director, who is most likely more concerned with the camera positions than with the actors' interpretations. This brevity of preparation helps explain why an actor must prepare carefully on his or her own before coming to the set and also helps to explain why type casting is so important in movies. Remember that Hollywood casting is based on choosing actors who already have the appearance and qualities appropriate for the roles. At first, all these deviations from the way one works in the theater are frustrating, but after a while the actor will begin to like film's approach. Some actors do their best work on camera.

Teaching an "Acting on Camera" class may be frustrating for the director/teacher at the beginning, since the techniques of filming are so different from the theater. Several weeks of working with the camera, along with careful observation of films and television to analyze how scenes are shot, edited, and framed, will soon develop the director's skills as a film-TV director.

With the advent of inexpensive and accessible video equipment on nearly every university or college campus, it is inevitable that "Acting on Camera" classes will become a regular part of the curriculum. Furthermore, it seems to me that it is the responsibility of a drama department to prepare its students for films and television since most of an actor's career derives from those mediums. Classes in "Acting on Camera" prepare the actor for this aspect of the performing arts and, just as the opportunities to appear in plays and musicals enhance an actor's skills, so does working on camera.

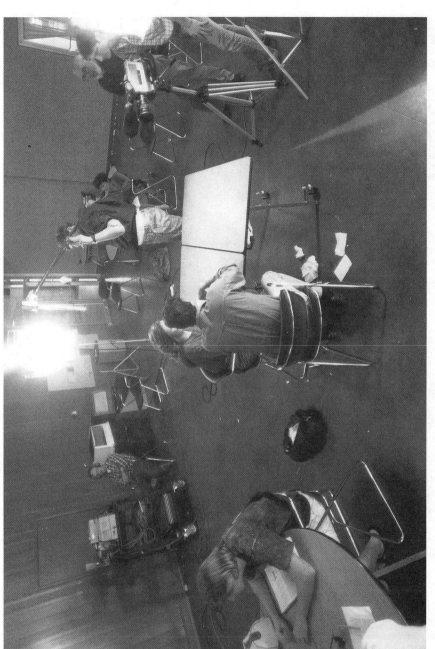

This photograph reveals several key components in the shooting of episode 1 from **BOYS AND GIRLS TOGETHER.** From left to right you can see an "atmosphere" person who will be seen in the background behind the two actors playing "Blake" and "Walt," in the left background a student who is operating the sound equipment, in the center foreground the two actors in the scene, right of them the sound boom operator (an actor doubling in brass as part of the crew), the director, and the cameraman. Usually the shooting will take place in a more cramped quarters and frequently with non-acting students milling around in the background. At such times we enlist acting students for crowd control.

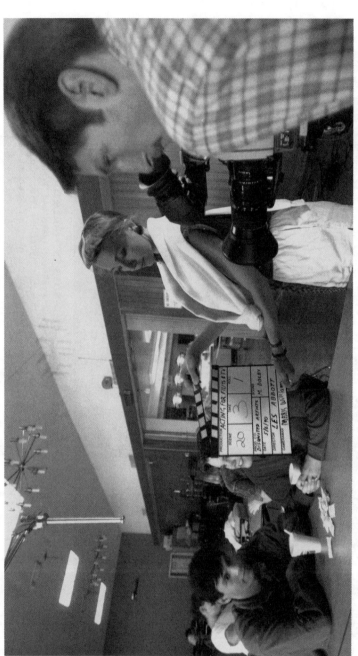

The two actors playing "Walt" and "Blake" are about to play a "two-shot" sequence from episode 1 of **BOYS AND GIRLS TOGETHER.** When this two-shot is complete the camera will be moved to behind Walt's right shoulder and then the same scene will be repeated as an "over-the-shoulder" shot of Blake from Walt's POV. Once that over-the-shoulder shot is completed the camera will be moved to where Walt's head is in the above picture and it will focus on Blake, who will then do her close-up of the same sequence. Walt will put his right eye as close to the camera's lens as he can so that Blake will be focused on him and not on the camera's lens. Each time the actors repeat this scene they must repeat their actions, picking up sugar packets, drinking coffee, reaching out and touching each other, exactly the same so that the editor can match up each of the shots as he/she picks and chooses from the two-shots, the over-the-shoulder shots, and the close-ups of the two actors. We shoot Blake's over-the-shoulder shot, and the close-up first since Walt has slightly more difficult material to play in this sequence and this gives him more opportunity to polish his characterization. Once the camera-man has said "mark it," the person on the slate-board says "Boys and Girls Together, scene 6, take 3" and then steps out of camera view. The director checks to see that there are no inappropriate extraneous elements such as a "mike-boom" or a background person staring at the action, and once he/she realizes that all is ready for the scene calls out "action!" Regardless of whatever mishaps may occur, the scene continues until the director calls out "cut!" Sometimes the cinematographer or the sound person may recognize that something is not going well and will need to call "cut!" The actors never stop the scene of their own volition.

The sound operator (an acting student whose assignment for the day is operating the sound equipment) for the day's shoot.

The director/teacher discusses a character point with the two actors who are playing "Walt" and "Blake" in episode 1 of **BOYS AND GIRLS TOGETHER.**

BOYS AND GIRLS TOGETHER

Episode 1
by
William Goldman

William Goldman, perhaps the highest paid screenwriter in Hollywood, began his career as a novelist. A prolific writer of more than 21 works, Goldman's novels include *The Temple of Gold, Marathon Man,* and *Your Turn to Curtsey, My Turn to Bow,* along with a fascinating non-fiction account of New York Theater called, *The Season: A Candid Look at Broadway* and an equally fascinating personal view of the film world and screenwriting entitled *Adventures in the Screen Trade.* Among his numerous screen credits are *Harper, Butch Cassidy and the Sundance Kid, All the President's Men,* and *The Princess Bride.*

Boys and Girls Together, Goldman's 1964 epic-scale novel, includes long episodes of dialog that richly reveal the dimensions of very diverse characters. From such a dialog episode, I have chosen sequences that reveal why Goldman's screenplays have been so successful. I purposely chose these particular sequences since they are suitable for many acting students whose age and experiences approximate those of the characters they are playing. Certainly college-age film acting students can quickly find experiences in their own lives that they can incorporate into their characterizations.

Nothing in the dialog from this first scene in *Boys and Girls Together* suggests the setting other than that it takes place on a college campus. For my purposes, I have broken the scene down into several campus settings simply to make it more interesting visually. When a director breaks down such a scene into different visual settings, it is part of his "shooting script." This scene could just as easily be played late at night as WALT brings BLAKE back to her sorority house, and the two deal with his frustration at not having been cast in a major role in the campus production. Another way the episode can be shot is in a day sequence with the actors sitting on a grassy knoll picnicking and, at the same time, dealing with Walt's sense of rejection at being passed over for the role. Other directors might find quite different but equally appropriate settings for this scene. The same kind of choice making in terms of settings can be made for other scenes included in *Acting for Films and TV*.

In breaking down the scene, I have arbitrarily chosen to move the characters through several closely approximated locales: the "green room" of a college playhouse, the stage and auditorium of the playhouse, a walkway across campus that leads to the cafeteria, and finally, several camera setups in the cafeteria itself. All of these locales enhance the visual aspect and the storytelling of what is, essentially, one scene. All the long shots do not have dialog and simply pick up whatever ambient sound there is in the atmosphere. The two characters' walking outdoors along the walkway is an example of how a director abbreviates time and suggests how characters get from one setting to another in the storytelling. I have also not used locales literally. When Walt storms through the door on the line, "Who does he think he is," from the way I have broken down the script it appears that he has started backstage and walked across the set of a play. The camera then pans into the auditorium as he strides across the stage and out the door of the theater. The locale used literally would have required that Walt go through five different doors to leave the theatre. The space is legitimized by this use without breaking up the action for the audience.

In Goldman's script we meet Walt, a bright, attractive but not handsome young man and his girl friend, Blake. She is a talented, spirited young woman who uses her wit to compensate for what she perceives to be her "plain Jane" looks. They are both students at an expensive university where he is majoring in theatre and she is majoring in English Literature. Walt is the son of a successful businessman who has amassed a fortune through his own grit and ruthlessness. The father is a philanderer whose blatant extramarital relations have caused Walt's mother considerable anguish. She is a quiet, affectionate, but ineffectual mother. Blake's mother and father divorced while she was a sophomore in high school. Both parents have since remarried and neither parent has given her much time, although Blake has always had every material comfort she might want. This is one of many ways that the scene might be staged for the camera:

INT. ACTORS' GREEN ROOM, JUST OFFSTAGE. DAY.

Several young actors are pushing towards the call board where the casting of *Hamlet* has just been posted. There is an exclamation of joy as two students learn that they have been cast. They move off frame as WALT and BLAKE move closer to the cast list. Walt runs his finger down the list of characters and the actors cast in each role. From Blake's attitude, it is obvious that she has learned about the casting through the grapevine. Walt fingers his way down the cast list until he finally spies his name.

                    WALT
                  (furious)

Osric! Me play Osric?

After a beat when she doesn't respond.

    Say something.

                    BLAKE

Something.

                    WALT

You're a scream, you are. Maybe it's a mistake. Do . . . Do you think it's a mistake?

                  (a beat)

That lousy director . . . who does he think he is?

Angrily Walt storms out of the door near the call board. Blake, resigned that it's going to be a rocky day, follows.

                                        CUT TO:

INT. BACKSTAGE AND ONSTAGE, CAMPUS PLAYHOUSE. DAY

WALT bangs through the door leading to the stage. From the camera's point of view (POV), we see him cross to a door leading into the interior stage set, stride across the stage as the camera pans with him, BLAKE following closely. In the background (bg) we see the empty theater seats. Walt leaps from the proscenium stage to the theater floor and strides through the first exit door. Blake follows him as well as she can.

                                                                    CUT TO:

EXT. PATH, CAMPUS. DAY

In a fury, WALT moves quickly down the path, BLAKE doing her best to keep up but lagging several steps behind him. They are moving towards the camera.

                                                                    CUT TO:

EXT. PATH, CAMPUS, DIFFERENT POV. DAY

We see WALT stride into a building with BLAKE following closely. The camera, shooting from the same position as the previous shot, sees their retreating backs as they enter the building.

                                                                    CUT TO:

INT: CAFETERIA COUNTER. DAY

Facing the camera is A STUDENT who is getting a drink. He moves out of the frame as WALT and BLAKE move into it. They get themselves cups of coffee during the dialog.

                              BLAKE

Hey, you're upset . . .

                              WALT

Nope.

Walt moves off frame, Blake following as another STUDENT pushes up to the coffee machine with

INT. CASHIER'S STATION, CAFETERIA. DAY.

The STUDENT just in front of WALT and BLAKE has finished paying for his drink. He moves out of the frame as Walt and Blake pass the CASHIER, Walt flinging the money down.

CUT TO:

INT. CONDIMENTS STATION, CAFETERIA. DAY.

A STUDENT pulls a napkin from a dispenser and heads for his table. WALT and BLAKE move into the frame. Walt grabs a bunch of sugar packets and a plastic stirrer as Blake exclaims,

BLAKE

Yes you are. You are too.

WALT

I'm not upset. It's just that I'm a senior and this is my last play and Osric . . . well, let's face it, Osric's just about the smallest part in the play. I mean, Osric! He's got about six stinking lines. Six lines.

Walt turns away from the condiments table in a fury. Blake looks as though she doesn't know what to do to mollify him, and then turns away from the condiments table.

CUT TO:

INT. CAFETERIA. DAY.

From a reverse angle, we see WALT and BLAKE walking towards a table. This could be a dolly shot with the camera approximately eight feet in front of them and moving with them as they head for a table.
  Spying an empty table they sit.

  Notes to the director/teacher and the actors:
    I have the camera dolly backwards in front of the actors, and
    I also have the camera pan with them as they move to their table,

which is to the left of the aisle between tables. A final camera move is that the camera tilts down with them as they sit. Since Walt sits last, the camera does not tilt down until he sits. Then, as the script shows, there is a cut to another POV with the camera lowered so there is a head-on two-shot of both actors.

CUT TO:

INT. TABLE, CAFETERIA. DAY

WALT and BLAKE are seated close to each other at the table. In the bg, we see other students and an occasional professor at other tables.

Notes to the director/teacher and the actors:

The remaining dialog in the scene is first shot in a master shot that includes both Walt and Blake in the shot. I make sure to move the camera several feet away from the dolly/pan shot position. Why? Although you would lower the camera on its pedestal for the two-shot of the actors sitting at the table if you kept the camera in the same position as in the prior sequence that included the dollying and panning shot, then you would get the effect of a "jump shot," which is disturbing to an audience, makes that audience extremely aware of the camera (which is bad story-telling) and is used only when a director chooses to shock the audience for some reason. By moving the camera to another position in addition to lowering the camera on its pedestal so that it is filming the characters straight on from their body-head positions, then the action of the characters will flow naturally and not be disturbing to the audience.

Once this master two-shot, including all the remaining dialog and the concluding embrace, has had a satisfactory take, then the camera moves for an over-the-shoulder shot that favors Blake from Walt's POV. When this shot is completed, including the ending embrace, I then have the camera placed where Walt has been sitting and we shoot Blake's close-ups. Walt positions himself so that his eyes are as close as possible to the camera's lens; Blake duplicates the same head actions she did in both the master-shot and the over-the shoulder shot of the sequence. Why do we shoot both Blake's over-the-shoulder shots and her close-ups before doing Walt's shots? In professional shoots, each camera shift of position takes time and, hence, is more costly. Shooting Blake's close-ups immediately after her over-the-shoulder shots requires minimum shifting of the camera and lights, saving money. Since this is a practical consideration in any professional shoot it should be practiced in student shoots as well. Once Blake's over-the-shoulder shots and close-ups have been completed, then the camera and lights are shifted and we shoot these same scenes favoring Walt from Blake's POV.

Each time we shoot the same dialog from a different camera position, the script supervisor and the director must be attentive to the actors' gestures and actions so that they match up when edited. If an actor drinks from a styrofoam cup between certain lines of dialog in the master shot, that action must be repeated exactly the same way in the over-the-shoulder shots and the close-ups. Actors need to become proficient in matching their action in the master shot to the over-the-shoulder shots and their close-ups so that the editor can match up all the action as he pieces together the various parts of each kind of shot when composing the sequential scene. Actors must learn to repeat the same actions consistently at exactly the same time, affording the editor more opportunities to give the actors a variety of shots in the final cut. The script supervisor's attention to these details is particularly important, since the director's attention is frequently split between various concerns that may cause him/her to miss such details.

The actors need to be cautioned not to overlap each other's dialog during any of the shots, since the editor needs to be able to cut cleanly from dialog in a two-shot to dialog in an over-the-shoulder shot to dialog in a close-up. If there are overlaps of dialog, punching up the action in a crucial moment through editing may not be possible. The opportunities for actors to get close-ups may also make the difference between a middling career and stardom.

WALT
(cont'd)

Well, I just won't play it, that's all. I mean, who does Hilton think he's dealing with, some freshman? I'm not remotely upset, but if you want to know the truth, when you audition to play Hamlet and get stuck with the smallest part in the play it's a little upsetting especially when you've played more leads than anybody else over the last four years, isn't that right? Who starred in CHARLEY'S AUNT, this fall?

BLAKE

That was a comedy, Egbert. You do comedy. HAMLET ain't supposed to be funny.

WALT

Well, if you were casting HAMLET would you have me play Osric?

BLAKE

Of course not.

WALT

Well, neither would I, so how come that crummy Hilton—

BLAKE
(interrupting)

Personally, I think you'd make a great Ophelia.

WALT

Will you just shut up!

BLAKE

Let's be honest . . . you're too young to play the Queen.

WALT

You know, whoever told you you were funny did us all a
vast disservice.

Notes to the director/teacher and the actors:
   *When the actors are preparing for this scene, even before
they get together for rehearsal a few minutes before the shoot,
they can learn something about their characters from the
dialog.   The preceding seven speeches can assist them in
developing their characters.   Blake's suggestion that Walt
would make "a great Ophelia" suggests that he is not the most
masculine of actors.   Perhaps that was the reason he was so
good in CHARLEY'S AUNT.   Walt's reaction to her funny
lines would suggest that he is all too aware that as an actor he
does not appear overly masculine.   Should we wonder about
Walt's sexual preference, however, that is clarified a few
moments later when Walt wonders "Why have I dated you all
year?" and Blake responds, "I think you keep hoping I'll put
out." All these speeches reveal the kind of people Walt and
Blake are.*

WALT
(cont'd)

I did one of those soliloquies for you. I wasn't bad. I
wasn't. Say that.

BLAKE

That.

WALT

Why have I dated you all year?

BLAKE

I think you keep hoping I'll put out.

WALT

I should have played Hamlet. I'm an actor.

> BLAKE
> (teasing)

My own little Bette Midler.

> WALT

Hey! Wait a minute. I've got a great idea!

> BLAKE

What?

> WALT

We'll do our own revue.

> BLAKE

Put on our own revue? Where'll we get the material?

> WALT

Write it. And what we can't write we'll steal from old Carol Burnett shows . . . I know about twenty sketches from that show that'll be great.

> (smiling)

And you know what else we'll do? We'll run it the same week as HAMLET and bankrupt them. Nobody casts me as Osric and gets away with it.

> BLAKE

Revues have songs, buddy.

> WALT

Well . . . you make up poems, don't you? You play the piano, right? Aren't you always blabbing about how creative you are? Write some songs.

> BLAKE

I have never, in my entire life, blabbed.

WALT

Will you write some songs, please? Better make them funny.

BLAKE

Aye, aye Sir. Right away Sir. Funny songs coming right up. Can we get Harold Prince to direct?

WALT

I'll direct the show, if you don't mind.

BLAKE

Ho-ho-ho.

WALT

Why do you always have to knock me? It so happens I'm one helluva director.

BLAKE

You've never directed anything in your life.

WALT

I have too.

BLAKE

What?

WALT

Plenty of things.

BLAKE

Name one.

WALT

That's not the point, don't you see? The point is, I've always wanted to be a director. I've thought about it. I've read about it. I know I can do it.

BLAKE

I thought you were an actor.

WALT

Acting... Who needs acting? As a matter of fact, if you want to know the truth, acting is a drag. It's not creative. You can't express yourself. All you do is spiel off something somebody else put down. But directing. That's something. In the immortal words of Katie Hepburn . . .

BLAKE

If you start with your imitations I'll throw up all over you.

WALT

You don't like my imitations?

BLAKE

I loathe your imitations.

WALT

Your name stinks.

BLAKE

Egbert Kirkaby don't ring bells, buddy.

WALT

You are smug, bitchy, and spoiled.

BLAKE

You're absolutely right. I'm a typical American girl. I also hate cooking, dread having children, intend cheating on my husband, and take the pill.

WALT

Why do you talk like that?

BLAKE

Rocks your foundation.

She grabs his hand and starts studying it like a Gypsy palm reader.

Your name is Walt Kirkaby and you wear glasses. You're a senior in college and getting duller every day. By the time you're thirty you'll think golf is the nuts, followed only slightly by gin rummy. By the time you're forty you'll be potbellied and you'll talk like Casanova in the men's locker room but you'll still be scared green every time you drop in the hay with a female.

Walt tries to pull his hand away. Blake holds tight.

And she won't always be your wife, this female. Your second wife, I should say, because you'll be on your second wife and your third kid by then, and your second wife won't be any better than your first one was, because you never wanted a woman in the first place. You wanted a servant, someone to darn—

WALT

Cut it!

BLAKE

So you'll get divorced and marry someone absolutely totally one hundred percent different except she'll be exactly the same only you won't know it until it's too late

and by that time you'll have figured out that all you
really wanted all your life was to bed down with your
mommy—

WALT

I said cut it—

She lowers her head, eyes closed, and kisses his palm again and again.
Suddenly, he senses her despair and it mingles with his. They lower
their heads together, holding on for dear life.

FADE OUT

BOYS AND GIRLS TOGETHER
Episode 2
by
William Goldman

DR. HELGA GUNTHER, a psychiatrist, heads a well-known New York City clinic. She is a jovial, levelheaded, intelligent woman of considerable compassion. AARON is a man in his mid twenties, handsome, intelligent, well educated. He works as a taxi driver in New York City. His educational background is not commensurate with his economic status nor the life he leads. Out of desperation, in despair for the self-destruction that seems to pervade his life, he has come to the clinic to attempt to get psychiatric help.

Notes to the director/teacher and actors:

This is a long scene, so I suggest that the scene be broken down into two acting groups with the first group starting the scene with Aaron's coming up the stairs and concluding with his line "O.K." in response to Dr. Gunther's statement, "Please stop saying 'I don't know' to questions we both know you know the answers to, O.K.?" The second group of actors may begin with Dr. Gunther's line, "Now you said you were robbed," and continue through to the last line of the scene, which should end on a fade out. This can usually be accomplished with a video camera.

The first and second groups may consist of four acting partnerships each, which means that eight men and eight women can be used in filming the sequence. It is always best to use several actors one right after the other in each camera setup, since that offers the actors more opportunities for on-camera time.

It should also be pointed out that Dr. Gunther may be played by either sex. Although William Goldman wrote the character as a man, the character could just as easily be played by a woman, as I have here, and indeed, a woman psychiatrist might make Aaron even more uneasy in this interview.

I wanted to create tension on Aaron's part before any dialog is spoken. For this reason I shoot this sequence on the second floor of a college building that has a conference room. This particular conference room has an oblong table approximately twelve feet long by four feet wide, which I place on a diagonal in the room. Diagonal objects help create a dramatic tension as opposed to symmetrical positioning, which helps to suggest serenity. Behind Dr. Gunther's chair, there should be several filing cabinets, so that at some time in the action, Dr. Gunther can use them to add physical activity to what is essentially a dialog scene bereft of action.

The action starts with Aaron's climbing the stairs to the second floor. He is apprehensive, and when he arrives at the top of the stairs, he leans against the wall for a long moment. He is considering whether to go into the interview with Dr. Gunther or flee. After a difficult moment of inner struggle, he resolves to see the psychiatrist. We see him walk down the hallway to the open door of the conference room, which represents Dr. Gunther's office. I usually have a couple of atmosphere people walk past him while he is going down the hall simply to add color to the action. Aaron stops at the doorway to Dr. Gunther's office. At this point, we cut to a medium shot of Dr. Gunther working on some papers at her desk.

She looks up when she sees the young man standing in the doorway.

GUNTHER

Aaron Fire?

Notes to the director/teacher and the actors:
A reverse shot from Dr. Gunther's point of view (POV), shows Aaron standing in the doorway. He nods, "Yes." We then cut back to Dr. Gunther's motioning to Aaron to come and sit beside her at the rectangular table. The empty chair is at a 45-degree angle from her chair. This enables both actors to be

shot in a two-shot with each actor given equal importance in the frame. We then cut to a shot of Aaron walking around the table to sit in the empty chair to Dr. Gunther's right. After he sits, we cut to a two-shot of both performers with the camera at least 45 degrees away from its previous position. We move the camera position at least this much to avoid the "jump cut" effect that happens when the shot cuts from one POV to another with the camera's positions not sufficiently distant from one another. From this two-shot camera position, we shoot both actors for the next 25 speeches.

AARON

I'm nervous.

Dr. Gunther nods.

I've never done anything like this before. I don't know where to begin.

GUNTHER

Well, why don't you begin with what brought you here.

AARON

What brought me here?

GUNTHER

Yes.

AARON

Well, I don't seem to be getting anywhere.

GUNTHER

Some days I feel that way, too.

(a beat)

Go on.

AARON

Well . . . well . . . I just don't seem to be getting anywhere, that's all.

GUNTHER

And that's what brought you here?

AARON

No, see, I was robbed. A couple of weeks ago. It upset me. I called the clinic the next day. But they couldn't give me an interview until today.

GUNTHER

There is nothing in this world so hard to find as an analyst in August.

There is a pause.

AARON

It's very hard. Just all of a sudden talking.

GUNTHER

Well, why don't you tell me about yourself? What do you do?

AARON

I'm a writer.

GUNTHER

A writer? Wonderful. Will you excuse a stupid question, but have you written anything I should have read?

AARON

No. I only wrote one book. *Autumn Wells,* I called it. It was rejected.

GUNTHER

When was this?

AARON

Three years ago.

GUNTHER

And everybody rejected it?

AARON

No. Just this one place. I never sent it out after that.

GUNTHER

Why?

AARON

I don't know. I meant to. I just never quite got around to doing it.

GUNTHER

And the past three years?

AARON

I . . . Nothing. Nothing.

GUNTHER

All right, we can come back to that. Tell me this. Where—

Notes to the director/teacher and the actors:
From this point forward until specified, I shoot this portion of the scene with over-the-shoulder shots, starting first with Dr. Gunther's action seen from Aaron's POV, and followed by Aaron's action seen from Dr. Gunther's POV. I choose this order of shooting the over-the-shoulder shots since I think

Aaron's acting is somewhat more demanding than Gunther's. We shoot his major on-camera work after we have shot Gunther's on-camera work.

AARON

(blurting) I went to the movies! O.K.? For three years I went to the movies. Everyday. Oh, I did other things, but mostly I just went to the movies. That's all. That's all.

GUNTHER

I hope for your sake you like them.

Aaron laughs.

AARON

Of course I like them. I'm not that crazy.

GUNTHER

I'll tell you if you're that crazy.

Gunther laughs.

You're embarrassed about it?

AARON

Wouldn't you be?

GUNTHER

Why did you go?

AARON

It passed the time. No . . . More than that. I don't know. I just went, that's all.

GUNTHER

And how did you afford this cinematic orgy?

AARON

Odd jobs, this and that.

GUNTHER

How odd is your present job?

AARON

I drive a taxi. On weekends. I have the last couple of years. It gets me by.

GUNTHER

Did you go to college?

AARON

Yes. Princeton.

GUNTHER

Finish?

AARON

Yes.

GUNTHER

How were your grades?

AARON

Good enough.

GUNTHER

Honors?

AARON

That's right.

Notes to the director/teacher and the actors:

Starting with the following line of dialog, I cut to close-ups, moving back and forth between the two actors. Why? This punches up the fact that Aaron is becoming more anxious because Dr. Gunther is beginning to bear down on him to get the kind of information she needs.

GUNTHER

I thought so.

(smiles)

Sometimes I'm terribly acute. Tell me, Mr. Fire, couldn't you have gotten a better job somewhere in the city?

AARON

I guess so. I tried one or two. I don't take orders very well.

GUNTHER

You were fired?

AARON

I was fired.

GUNTHER

Did that please you?

AARON

. . . I don't understand.

GUNTHER

Let it pass. Where do you live now?

AARON

West Eighty-Fourth Street. Between Amsterdam and Columbus.

GUNTHER

Of your own choice?

AARON

Yes.

GUNTHER

That's supposed to be the worst street in the city.

AARON

Yes. You bet it is.

GUNTHER

Is that why you live there?

AARON

What does that mean?

GUNTHER

What do you think it means?

AARON

I live there . . . I live there because when I was looking for
a place there was a place that I could afford so I took it,
O.K. ?

GUNTHER

O.K.

AARON

I'm sorry.

GUNTHER

For what?

AARON

I shouldn't have talked to you like that.

GUNTHER

Why shouldn't you?

(a beat)

Because you're afraid I won't like you and if I don't like you I won't recommend you for the clinic, is that it?

AARON

Yes.

GUNTHER

Mr. Fire, the last person I recommended was a young man who was practically a carbon copy of my first husband whom I loathed beyond belief. Does that make you feel any better?

AARON

Yes.

GUNTHER

Swear at me if you want to . . . Do anything you want, except please stop saying, "I don't know" to questions we both know you know the answers to, O.K.?

AARON

O.K.

Notes to the director/teacher and the actors:

At this point, if two teams of actors are performing this scene, the second team of actors may take over from the first team. In my shooting of this next sequence, I shoot medium shots, first of Dr. Gunther, who goes to her filing cabinet and pulls out a folder, and then of Aaron as he might be seen from Gunther's POV at the filing cabinet.

GUNTHER

Now you said you were robbed.

AARON

Yes.

GUNTHER

Who robbed you?

AARON

Some guy.

GUNTHER

Where did this happen?

AARON

Over near Ninth Avenue. Between Ninth and Tenth. At night.

GUNTHER

A slum area.

AARON

Yes.

GUNTHER

You were walking alone through this slum area at night and some guy robbed you.

AARON

Yes.

Notes to the director/teacher and the actors:
At this point, I have Dr. Gunther pull out a file and em-
phatically slam the drawer shut. She walks back to her seat at

the table; she is zeroing in on Aaron and pushing for information.

GUNTHER

Are you lying?

AARON

Yes.

GUNTHER

Please, Fire.

AARON

I don't want to talk about the robbery.

GUNTHER

That's a hell of a thing to tell an analyst. "I don't want to talk about it."

AARON

I don't. It's not important.

GUNTHER

You just finished saying it was what brought you here.

AARON

I was probably lying again.

GUNTHER

Do you lie a lot?

AARON

Yes, yes, all the ti—. No! I don't lie. I never lie! . . . Except sometimes I do.

Notes to the director/teacher and the actors:
Beginning with the following line, I cut back and forth with close-ups of the two characters. Directors frequently cut from one kind of shot to another to point up questions and, more specifically, to point up a new beat (such as a new idea).

GUNTHER

Did you report the robbery?

AARON

Hell no.

GUNTHER

I would have if I'd been robbed. I would have gone to the police. Why didn't you?

AARON

Are you trying to insinuate something?

Gunther simply watches, saying nothing.

Look . . . I didn't report it because I didn't have much money on me so what was the point because who wants to get mixed up with the cops when you don't have to anyway?

Notes to the director/teacher and the actors:
I use a two-shot of the actors when I shoot this section of the scene. Again, this change of the camera's position is partly motivated by the need to show Dr. Gunther's writing something down on a notepad and Aaron's almost paranoid reaction to Dr. Gunther's action. It is also motivated because this is the beginning of a new beat.

Gunther jots something down on a piece of paper.

AARON
(cont'd)

What are you doing? . . . What are you writing down there? Is it about me? What are you writing about me?

GUNTHER

Anyone ever tell you you're suspicious?

AARON

What did you write down about me?

GUNTHER

It's a reminder to myself to pick up my husband's clothes at the cleaners.

Hands Aaron the paper.

AARON

No. I'm sorry.

GUNTHER

What did you think I was writing?

AARON

What do you know about me?

GUNTHER

Just what you told me. Precious little.

AARON

I thought you were putting down something about me . . . you never know what a shrink is thinking.

GUNTHER

What in the world are you afraid of?

AARON

I'm not afraid of anything . . . I'm not. Not of anything.

Gunther smiles.

You're the suspicious one. Not me. Can we get a little
air in here?

GUNTHER
(gestures to window)

Help yourself.

Aaron goes to the window, raises it.

Notes to the director/teacher and the actors:
One way of shooting the following section of the scene is to
cut the action back and forth, first from one character's POV
and then from the other character's POV. I suggest shooting
the medium shots of Dr. Gunther from Aaron's POV at the
windows first, then the same sequence from Gunther's POV.
Again, we shoot the actor with the more demanding dialog and
action second: in this case, Aaron.

AARON

There. That's a lot better. Central Park. You take the
rest of the city, just leave me Central Park.

GUNTHER

How long have you lived here?

AARON

Three years.

GUNTHER

And you don't like it?

AARON

I hate it.

GUNTHER

Why don't you leave?

AARON

Leave New York?

GUNTHER

It's been done.

AARON

I couldn't. I just couldn't. You come to New York, you don't leave. They're all from Kansas City or Pittsburgh, or Roanoke, Virginia. But they come here. They don't like it here. You're not supposed to like it here. But you gotta come anyway. It's the place. New York's the place. But you're not supposed to like it.

GUNTHER

And you came here to be a writer?

AARON

Yes.

GUNTHER

Are you a good writer?

Aaron says nothing.

We haven't much time. Now come back and sit down and tell me.

Notes to the director/teacher and the actors:
From a different camera position, which will become a two shot of Aaron and Dr. Gunther, we shoot Aaron as he leaves the window and comes back to the table and sits. The camera pans with him as he makes this move, and when the camera stops panning, it is because he is seated beside Dr. Gunther.

AARON

I don't know. I used to think I was. Once, I was positive. Now I don't know anymore.

GUNTHER

These past three years—have you written?

AARON

It's hard to write here. To concentrate, I mean. There's so much to do.

GUNTHER

What did you do? I know, you went to the movies. Besides that?

AARON

I wrote a little. Not much. Nothing really. I don't know. Things. Like that.

GUNTHER

Social life?

AARON

Oh, sure. I went out with a lot of girls. I did that. I dated plenty.

GUNTHER

Read?

AARON

Sure. No, not so much. Like I said, it's hard to concentrate, there's so much to do.

GUNTHER

What are you afraid of?

AARON

Nothing.

Notes to the director/teacher and the actors:
At this point Gunther is beginning really to pressure Aaron.
The psychiatrist is forcing the young man to stop evading the
truth and tell her why he wants to be admitted to the clinic.
Consequently, I think it advisable to cut back and forth be-
tween the two characters with close-ups, perhaps each cut
revealing the character in increasingly tighter framing.

GUNTHER

I've had that answer. What are you afraid of?

AARON

Not you! I'll tell you that. Not you and your stupid
questions.

GUNTHER

Then why don't you answer them?

AARON

I will! Ask me anything! I'll answer it. Go ahead. Ask
me anything!

GUNTHER

Why didn't you report the robbery to the police?

Aaron laughs.

Notes to the director/teacher and the actors:
As Aaron laughs nervously, I have him get up and move
away from Dr. Gunther. He has a tremendous need to get
breathing space between him and the psychiatrist. He moves to
the wall at the other end of the table so that when he leans on the
wall he is facing Dr. Gunther across the table. We cut back and
forth between the two characters. These are medium shots,
since we want to emphasize that the two characters are at
opposite ends of the room. When we shoot Dr. Gunther, we see

her from Aaron's standing POV, while when we shoot Aaron, we see him from Dr. Gunther's sitting POV. The camera should always see the action from the character's POV.

AARON

I know what you're thinking. And you're wrong. As a matter of fact, I'm living with this girl right now. A dancer. She's a dancer and as far as sex is concerned she's practically a nymphomaniac and I'm the first guy she's found who can satisfy her. In her whole life, the first guy.

GUNTHER

How long have you been living with her?

AARON

Eight, nine months; going on a year.

GUNTHER

You plan to marry her?

AARON

Hell no.

GUNTHER

Why not?

AARON

She's a Spic. Her name's Chita. You just can't go around marrying a girl named Chita. What do you think my mother would do if I brought some girl named Chita home to marry? Boy, that's funny if I brought old Chita home. Not that there's anything wrong with the way she looks, you understand. She's great looking. She's got this incredible body, not skinny like most dancers. I mean, she's got these great breasts and a real ass on her. But she's lithe like a dancer. The things she can do with her body. You wouldn't believe what she can do. And her face is pretty. Big black eyes and a nasty mouth. And she's smart, too. Not one of those dumb spics. She had two years of college—she majored in English—she reads all the time. That's how we met, because of the reading. See, I carry a book with me in the cab and she got in and she had a book, too, and she said was I reading that book—it was CRIME AND PUNISHMENT by Dostoevski—and I said I was and she said that was funny because most cab drivers don't read and I pointed at her book and said neither did most Puerto Ricans and we both laughed and she gave me her name and when I got off duty I called her and we went for a walk in Central Park, talking about this and that, books mostly, and when we were done walking we went to her place and she said she really liked me but she wasn't sure we ought to shack up on account of her being, like I said, almost a nymphomaniac that nobody could satisfy but I told her I was the boy so we hit the sack and she was a tiger growling and clawing at me but I stayed with her right to the end riding her down and afterwards she kissed me like a baby and kept saying I was right, I was her boy, over and over, I was her boy . . .

Notes to the director/teacher and the actors:

Somewhere about here in Aaron's long speech I suggest that the actor move from the wall, which he has unconsciously used as a kind of emotional crutch, up to the end of the long table so that he puts his hands on the table to support himself as he faces Dr. Gunther. When Aaron arrives at the end of the line,.".. she loves me and brings me presents and is great looking with two years of college and . . .," he can no longer look at the doctor. Holding onto the table for support, his whole body sinks in despair. Finally, after a long moment, he looks up at Gunther and says, "It's not ringing true, is it?" Following his admission that he is a homosexual and the plea, "Why is that," the scene should fade slowly to black.

AARON
(cont'd)

She loves me something awful, waits on me, does what I tell her, wants to marry me . . . she really is a great thing, smart and gorgeous but its strictly a bed relationship, what we have, at least as far as I'm concerned, that's all it can ever be, strictly a bed relationship, even though she loves me and brings me presents and is great looking with two years of college and . . .

(a beat)

It's not ringing true, is it?

GUNTHER

I don't know. Is it?

AARON

No.

(a long pause)

I'm homosexual. Why is that?

FADE OUT

MANHATTAN
by
Woody Allen

Woody Allen first came to national attention as a stand-up comedian. His droll accounts as one of the world's great losers, and reliance on psychiatric analysis touched a responsive chord in an audience traumatized by the upheavals of the sixties. His comic observations in *The New Yorker* magazine gained him an even larger audience. His first movies gave little hint that he would become the most creative, original filmmaker currently working in motion pictures. Beginning with *Annie Hall* and continuing with *Manhattan, Interiors, The Purple Rose of Cairo, Zelig, Hannah and her Sisters,* and *Radio Days,* Allen has continued to astound us with his imaginative chronicles of our life and times.

PENNY and BOB are part of that group of people today's newspapers describe as "singles." They are urbane, sophisticated, well educated, knowledgeable, reasonably affluent, lonely, and unmarried. In matters of the heart both people are fearful of marriage, doubtful about the possibilities of long-lasting, meaningful relationships, and imbued with this age's sense of alienation. Penny has given a party for her group of friends and Bob, whom she does not know very well, has remained as the rest of the group is leaving. As the action begins, they are standing in the doorway of Penny's apartment bidding good-bye to the group. Both have entertained the notion that their relationship should move past "hardly know each other" to "know each other in the biblical sense," but neither has voiced this notion. Bob has remained with some sort of faint hope that Penny might ask him to stay the night. He has been dating an eighteen year old girl.

Notes to the director/teacher and the actors:
Again, this sequence can be shot in one of those relatively utilitarian apartments you find near every campus. The opening shot is a wide-angled profile shot of Penny and Bob

standing in the doorway of an apartment, saying goodnight to some of Penny's party guests. There is an ad lib of "good-byes" as the two watch the partygoers go down the hall. Then, when the guests are out of earshot, Bob speaks.

BOTH

Good-night. Bye-bye.

BOB

Some interesting group of people your friends are.

Notes to the director/teacher and the actors:

The camera is positioned inside the living room so that as Penny and Bob come into the living room and Penny closes the door, Bob is saying, "Some interesting group of people your friends are." Penny responds with, "I know," as she starts picking up cocktail glasses and moves towards the kitchen. Taking his cue from Penny, Bob starts picking up some leftover hors d'oeuvres and follows her into the kitchen. As she puts the dirty glasses on the kitchen sink, he puts the hors d'oeuvres on the kitchen table and sits in a chair at the table. He then continues with, "Yeah, how come you guys got divorced? That's something I never . . ." Penny turns from the counter to repond, and we have a series of medium-close shots back and forth between the two that continue until Bob has said, ". . . because my ex-wife left me for another woman." At this point we cut to a profile two-shot of Bob and Penny as she comes over to the table, sitting as she responds, "Really?" This two-shot continues through Bob's line, "I tried to run them both over with a car." After that it cuts back and forth between the two, who are now seated opposite each other at the kitchen table.

PENNY

I know.

BOB

The cast of a Fellini movie.

PENNY

They're such fun. They're such wonderful people, and Helen is really a good friend. She's a very brilliant woman, you know. She's really a genius. I met her through my ex-husband, Jerome.

BOB

Yeah, how come you guys got divorced? That's something I never . . .

PENNY

Well, I don't understand, what do you mean how come we got divorced? What kind of question is that? I hardly even know you at all.

BOB

You don't have to tell me really. I'm just curious.

PENNY

Oh well, we had a lot of problems. We fought a lot. I was tired of submerging my identity to a very brilliant, dominating man. He was a genius.

BOB

He was a genius. Helen is a genius, and Dennis is a genius. You know a lot of geniuses. You should meet some stupid people once in awhile; you can learn something.

PENNY

Okay . . . well, tell me: Why did you get a divorce?

BOB

Why? I got a divorce because my ex-wife left me for another woman.

PENNY

Really?

BOB

Uh huh.

PENNY

God, that must have been really demoralizing.

BOB

Well, I don't know. I think I took it very well under the circumstances.

PENNY

Whooo-wheee.

BOB

I tried to run them both over with a car.

PENNY

I can imagine. I mean, that's incredible sexual humiliation. It's enough to turn you off of women, and I think it accounts for the little girl.

BOB

The little girl's fine. Jesus! I mean, what's with the little girl?

PENNY

Sure I understand, believe me, sixteen years old, no possible threat at all.

BOB

She's eighteen, she's going to be . . . you know sometimes you have a losing personality, Penny.

Notes to the director/teacher and the actors:
   The camera, from Bob's seated POV, tilts up as Penny gets up on her line, "Hey, I'm honest. . . ." From another camera position, we see Penny heading towards the living room. Bob follows her, saying, "And I like the way you express yourself, you know."

PENNY

Hey, I'm honest. What do you want? I say what's on my mind and if you can't take it, well then fuck off!

BOB

And I like the way you express yourself, you know. It's pithy yet degenerate. Do you get many dates? I don't think so.

Notes to the director/teacher and the actors:
   Penny turns back, facing Bob, and we hear her answer from Bob's POV, "No? I do. I actually . . . now I do. You'll never believe this, but I never thought I was very pretty." We cut to another camera position in the living room, and the camera pans with her as she moves to the sofa. The camera tilts down with her as she sits on the line, "It's all so subjective anyway." Bob moves into the frame and sits beside her on his line, "Yeah."

PENNY

No? I do. I actually . . . now I do. You'll never believe this, but I never thought I was very pretty. Oh, what is pretty anyway? I hate being pretty. It's all so subjective anyway.

BOB

Yeah.

PENNY

I mean the brightest men just drop dead in front of a beautiful face and the minute you climb into the sack, if you're the least bit giving, they're so grateful.

BOB

Yeah, I know I am.

PENNY

Do you have any kids or anything like that?

BOB

Yes. I've got a kid. He's being raised by two women at the moment.

PENNY

Oh, you know, I think that works. They've made studies. I read in one of the psychoanalytic quarterlies, kids don't need a male. Two mothers are absolutely fine.

BOB

Really? I always feel very few people survive one mother.

Notes to the director/teacher and the actors:

Penny gets up after Bob's line, "I always feel very few people survive one mother." She heads towards her bedroom door on her "Hmmmm . . .," and then turns back as she says, ". . . oh, listen. I got to get my dog. Do you want to wait? I've got to walk it. Are you in a rush or something like that?" Then we cut back and forth between the two characters as they speak from their respective POVs, through Bob's line, "Oh, I would have thought that in your case a Great Dane." Then, as Penny starts for the bedroom, the camera picks her up from another position, at least 45 degrees away from the prior camera position. We cut to a close-up of Bob as he asks, "So are you serious with 'Yale' or what?" At the door she turns, and from Bob's POV, we hear her response.

PENNY

Hmmm . . . oh, listen, I got to get my dog. Do you want to wait? I've got to walk it. Are you in a rush or something like that?

BOB

No. I mean sure. What kind of dog do you got?

PENNY

The worst. It's a dachshund . . . you know it's a penis substitute for me.

BOB

Oh, I would have thought that in your case a Great Dane.

Heading towards the bedroom.

PENNY

Ha, ha, ha. I'll go get the dog.

BOB

So are you serious with "Yale" or what?

She turns.

PENNY

Serious with "Yale?" He's married. Uh, I don't know . . . I guess I think I should straighten my life out. Donny, my analyst, is always telling me . . .

BOB

You call your analyst Donny?

PENNY

Yeah, I call him Donny. Ha ha.

Notes to the director/teacher and the actors:
We continue cutting back and forth from one character to another, and from Bob's POV, Penny moves back to the sofa as she says, ". . . I mean . . . especially with my ex-husband Jerome." She sits on the sofa facing towards him as she continues, "I was a student and um . . ." We then cut back and forth in close-ups from each one's POV from one character to the other.

BOB

Donny, your analyst. I call mine Dr. Chomski. You know he hits me with a ruler . . . Donny.

PENNY

Anyway, Donny tells me I get involved in these situations and that it's deliberate, ya know . . . I mean . . . especially with my ex-husband, Jerome. I was a student and um . . .

BOB

Really! You married your teacher.

PENNY

Yeah, of course.

BOB

That's very, very . . .

PENNY

Well, listen. He failed me and I fell in love with him.

BOB

That's perfect . . . that's perfect.

PENNY

I know perfect right. I was sleeping with him and he had the nerve to give me an F.

BOB

Well, really.

PENNY

Yeah, really.

BOB

Not even an incomplete, right? Just a straight F.

PENNY

Ha ha. You know you have a good sense of humor, you actually do.

BOB

Hey thanks. I don't need you to tell me that, you know. I've been making good money off it for years till I quit my job to write this book and now I'm very, very nervous about it.

Notes to the director/teacher and the actors:
Penny gets up from the sofa just before she says, "Do you want to go walk by the river?" We cut to a different camera position for a two-shot, as Bob stands up saying, "Do you know what time it is now?" The camera should be positioned near the bedroom door so that as they talk, they walk towards the camera, and then past the camera to enter the bedroom. The camera then cuts to another position, showing Bob following Penny into the bedroom on his line, "I could talk about my book all night."

PENNY

Do you want to go walk by the river?

BOB

Do you know what time it is now?

PENNY

What do you mean?

BOB

If I don't get at least sixteen hours, I'm a basket case.

PENNY

I'd like to hear about your book, I really would. I'm quite a good editor.

BOB

Yeah?

PENNY

Uh huh.

BOB

Well, my book is about decaying values. It's about . . . see . . . the thing is . . . years ago I wrote a short story about my mother, called "The Castrating Zionist," and I want to expand it into a novel. You know . . . I could talk about my book all night . . .

They are walking into the bedroom.

FADE OUT

A CLEARING IN THE WOODS
Episode 1
by
Arthur Laurents

Arthur Laurents' career in both theatre and films has been so impressive that it is difficult to list all his credits. The playwright-director first came to the attention of theatre-lovers with his powerful drama about racial discrimination, *Home of the Brave*. Among his other plays are *The Time of the Cuckoo, The Bird Cage, Invitation to a March,* and *A Clearing in the Woods*. His accomplishments also include the librettos for two Broadway musical classics, *West Side Story* and *Gypsy*. Many critics consider *Gypsy* to have the best book of any musical ever produced.

Laurents' recent films include *The Way We Were* and *The Turning Point,* and other screenplays written by the prolific writer include *Anastasia, The Snake Pit,* and *Rope*. In recent years, Laurents has added directing to his credits with the staging of *La Cage aux Folles* and the brilliant revival of *Gypsy*.

PETE and GINA are husband and wife. They met in college where Gina was an excellent student and Pete was an average student who was a "big man on campus," mostly because of his prowess on the athletic field.

EXT. A CLEARING IN THE WOODS. NIGHT.

For a moment the woods are empty of human activity. Then suddenly we see PETE running into the clearing. He is panting from the exertion of running. Barechested, he has been carrying a shirt which he flings to the ground in frustration. Then he sits on a rock his body rocking with despair. After a moment he is joined by GINA who is wearing a hastily put on dressing gown.

> *Notes to the director/teacher and the actors:*
> *This scene works better if shot at night, not only because it is the time when the scene takes place, but also because you can*

control the lighting better at a night shooting. This results in a more effective scene. Three different sources of artificial lighting should give the best results. The opening sequence should be a long shot of Pete, running into the clearing in the woods. After he is seated or crouched on the ground, his body rocking with frustration, we should see Gina run in behind him so that he doesn't see her until she speaks.

GINA

There's no place you can go at this hour, Pete. Come back to the house.

(a beat)

I'll sleep in Father's study.

PETE

Do you want a divorce?

GINA

Of course not!

Notes to the director/teacher and the actors:
   Peter never looks at Gina once she has spoken, but says his line facing the camera: "Do you want a divorce?" Gina answers, "Of course not," standing. Then she crouches down slightly behind him to say, "Pete, what happened isn't so terrible—" The camera should cut to another position at least 45 degrees away from its prior position right after she crouches.

GINA
(cont'd)

Pete, what happened isn't so terrible—

PETE

Gina, I don't want to talk about it—

GINA

Or even so unusual.

Notes to the director/teacher and the actors:

The dialog from ". . . isn't so terrible" through "Or even so unusual," should be delivered with Pete in the foreground (fg) of the frame with Gina seen over his shoulder, somewhat behind him. This staging technique is always very effective on camera but is, at first, difficult for stage-trained actors to accept. They feel that they should be making eye contact with their acting partner; but psychologically, it may be difficult for the two characters to look at each other. This method of shooting helps communicate this difficulty. Watch films and you will soon learn that this is a frequently used device, which you, as an audience, have never questioned.

PETE

Gina—

GINA

It happens to most men.

PETE

How often?   And afterwards, breathing evenly to act asleep.

GINA

There's no need for details.

Notes to the director/teacher and the actors:

As Pete says, "Gina—," he should turn to face her. A clever editor will show the turn, starting from the previous camera position and then finishing the cut from the camera's new position, which should be at least 45 degrees from the previous camera position and with the camera pedestal lowered to the crouched actors' eye level. This dialog should continue, cutting back and forth between the two actors, each being seen from each other's POV with the camera pedestal lowered through the line, "There's no need for details." This scene has many camera positions and cuts, since the material is highly dramatic and catches two characters at a moment of tremendous tension in their lives; the fast cuts and the many camera positions help to define the building anxiety in both characters.

PETE

And the excuses in the morning: "Gee, I was awfully tired last night; gee, I was awfully drunk last night." When we both know—

GINA

Don't you know it's humiliating for me, too. To know that I don't excite you anymore. That you don't find me attractive any more.

Notes to the director/teacher and the actors:
  Pete should rise and move away from Gina on the line, "And the excuses in the morning." We should cut from the previous camera angle to another angle, so that Pete seems to be walking towards the camera (actually only two or three steps), and so that the upper part of his body and his face fill the left side of the frame. Gina follows him, so she is standing behind his left shoulder and fills the right side of the frame, on her line, "Don't you know it's humilating ..." As Pete turns towards her on his line, "I do. It isn't that," we begin a series of cuts back and forth with over-the-shoulder shots.

PETE

I do. It isn't that.

GINA

Then what is it?

PETE

All I know is that I've disappointed you.

GINA

It's you who are disappointed in me.

PETE

You always think that.

GINA

With reason!

PETE

What do you mean?

GINA

You only married me because we thought I was going to have a baby.

PETE

That's wild! We had it all arranged to be married right after graduation.

GINA

We never set a definite date until we thought I was pregnant. Even the doctor thought I was. You'll have to admit that. Even he didn't know it was a false pregnancy and you spoke to him yourself, so—

PETE

What are you doing?

GINA

Well—

PETE

What's wrong with me is not because I think you trapped me into marriage. I never thought that!

GINA

It never crossed your mind?

PETE

No.

Notes to the director/teacher and the actors:
The camera should be set 45 degrees away from its last over-the-shoulder position. From this new position, we pick up a two-shot of the actors, and Gina turns towards the camera's new position just before she says, "But why did you marry me?" Pete is slightly behind her and seen over her shoulder in the medium two-shot, encompassing the actors from head to toe, as the two continue their dialog through Gina's line, "I was somebody, too." Following this line, we have a series of close-ups of both actors, their faces nearly filling the frame.

GINA

But why did you marry me? You were the biggest man on campus: letter man, council president—

(proudly)

remember—the school voted you "Man of the Year"—

PETE

Too bad you can't retire at 20.

GINA

I still remember what it felt like to walk into a dance with you, wearing your pin. Or when we met in a corridor, or walked across the campus. I caught your glow and spread it around me in front of all of them. I was somebody, too.

PETE
(a discovery)

Is that why you married me?

GINA

Would that be so wrong?

PETE

Gina—tell me what it feels like to walk into a dance with me now, wearing my ring.

GINA

You look for the wrong meanings.

PETE

But the biggest man on campus doesn't walk through doors now; he can walk right under them—stretched to his full height! His big job now is playing golf with his wife's father!

GINA

I happen to like my father!

PETE

So do I—

GINA

I don't mean I want you to become like him—

PETE

Then why did you badger me into quitting the one real job I've had since school?

GINA

It wasn't good enough for you.

PETE

Apparently the jobs that are good enough I'm not good enough to get.

GINA

You are!

PETE

Then why don't I get them?

GINA

You will!

PETE

When?

GINA

When you stop swimming laps and doing push-ups and going to games; when you stop being a boy!

She is horrified by the onrush of words that has caused her to make this disclosure. Pete can see how she really feels about him. It takes a moment for him to digest it.

Notes to the director/teacher and the actors:
Once the camera has registered Gina's horror at the realiza-tion that she has spoken far too brutally to her husband, the camera should cut to a two-shot of the actors. This time the camera should be much closer, so that both actors appear in the frame from slightly above the waist and their heads fill the frame.

PETE

Meaning when I stop living off of you.

GINA

I never said that!

PETE

But it's true and I'm ashamed of it! I'm ashamed of taking from you and not being able to—not standing on my—not being up to what—I'm strangling on the double meanings!

GINA

That whole subject is nothing to—

PETE

And before I said, "Standing stretched to full height" when in my mind it was standing erect—

GINA

Pete, please—!

There's a moment's silence, both are embarrassed.

PETE

One thing about jobs. I know you really want more and can do more than this welfare work you—

GINA

I only want to help you.

PETE

Gina, I'm drowning! Maybe you think you're helping me to shore but you can't swim yourself. You keep telling me you fell in love with the biggest man on campus. Well, school's out and the world's in. I'm nothing!

GINA

That's not so!

PETE

It is. But it doesn't have to stay that way. Maybe I can't be man of the year but I can be something if you help.

GINA

I want to.

PETE

Help me get started to being even a little something.

GINA

I don't know what to do anymore. I've tried—I have—

Notes to the director/teacher and the actors:
At this point, we cut to over-the-shoulder shots of the two
actors, cutting back and forth on each actor's lines. This
choice helps build the scene to its climax—both characters'
emotions are out of control; in the future both of them will
replay this scene in their heads and wonder what they might
have done differently.

PETE
(a discovery)

But you've given up. Just as you have with—with what I
suppose I was really talking about. With making love.

GINA

I have not! I told you: it's just as bad for me—It's no
different for a woman.

PETE

Yes, it is. A woman can fake.

GINA

Fake?!

PETE

You do. You have.

GINA

That's crazy.

PETE

I can tell when I hold you in my arms.

GINA

How like you to blame me!

PETE

And when I fail, I think you're glad!

GINA

You can't actually believe that. How dare you even think it!

PETE

I haven't; I just guessed. Gina, you're glad!

GINA

You'd better stop that—

PETE

Admit it!

GINA

No!

PETE

The truth!

GINA

Truth doesn't exist!

PETE

Skip the fancy evasions. The truth!

GINA

What's true for you is not true for me!

PETE

Then just what is true for you!?

GINA
(an outburst)

I don't know anymore!

Pete realizes that both of them are in too much trouble to mend this marriage.

Notes to the director/teacher and the actors:
Cut back to a close-up of Pete's reacting to Gina's outburst, "I don't know any more!" Then cut to a tight medium shot of both characters in profile.
After a moment:

PETE

I do want a divorce—before I do drown.

GINA

Are you serious?

PETE

Unless there is something you want to say.

GINA

I'm not going to beg, if that's what you mean. I have too much pride for that.

PETE

How can you have pride and still be in love?

GINA

How can you destroy respect and still ask for love?

PETE

It's pretty silly to stand here and insult one another.

GINA

Very. Shall we just say good-bye?

PETE
(reluctantly)

O.K. Good-bye, Gina.

He starts to make a move, almost as if he wants to take her into his arms but she reaches out to shake his hand.

GINA

Good-bye.

Notes to the director/teacher and the actors:
   From a different camera position, we see both Gina and Pete in a long shot. He walks back into the woods and disappears. After a moment, we see Gina rush to the edge of the woods where Pete has gone.

He goes off into the trees; she stands still for a moment and then suddenly runs to the edge of the clearing.

Notes to the director/teacher and the actors:
   In a medium-close shot at the edge of the clearing, we see Gina calling after Pete. Once she has called to him and there is no answer, the scene fades out.

GINA
(cont'd)

Pete!

She waited a moment too long; she realizes that he doesn't hear her.

FADE OUT

A CLEARING
IN THE WOODS
Episode 2
by
Arthur Laurents

NORA and HAZELMAE are two teenagers whose parents are wealthy. They are, for the moment, "best friends." Nora is spirited, somewhat rebellious, keenly bright, and will soon blossom into an attractive young woman. Her real name is Virginia but she has chosen to call herself "Nora" after the heroine of Henrik Ibsen's *A DOLL'S HOUSE*. Hazelmae hasn't quite lost her baby fat and her weight problem may be a lifetime burden; she affects a too-thick southern accent. Although she tries to be independent, Hazelmae lacks a sense of adventure and will always be, ultimately, a conformist. THE BOY is a "townie": that is, someone who lives in the small New England town whose one claim to fame is that it is the locale of the celebrated girls' school. His parents are lower middle class. He is an attractive, well-built young man, quick-witted and cognizant of his teenage sex appeal. Someday he will escape the confines of his narrow environment and live an interesting life. The scene takes place in a clearing in the woods where the two girls are going to picnic.

Notes to the director/teacher and the actors:
    None of the suggested ways of shooting these scenes is sacrosanct. They are simply ways of approaching the material, and each director may have a different notion of what is important within the scene. Frames and shots should be chosen accordingly. I start this scene with a long shot showing a green countryside (most campuses have at least a few such locales) with Nora's moving towards the camera, while far in the background (bg) we see a huffing and puffing Hazelmae. Nora, carrying a basket and a blanket, turns around to face the lagging Hazelmae. As soon as she turns in the long shot, we cut to a medium shot of her facing the slower Hazelmae.

NORA
(shouting)

Hazelmae! Hazelmae!

Notes to the director/teacher and the actors:
  From Nora's POV, we see Hazelmae, carrying a cosmetic case and a couple of pillows, struggling though the woods. Then we cut back to Nora, who turns away from the camera, spies a good picnic spot, and starts to put the blanket down with the picnic basket. After a few moments, Hazelmae will enter the medium-shot frame and start her dialog.

HAZELMAE

I declare, Nora lamb, over hill and dale to this? It certainly isn't my idea of chic.

Both girls settle on the blanket as their conversation continues. After a moment Hazelmae will open her cosmetic case, take out a mirror and tweezers, and set to work.

NORA

Nature, honey lamb, is not chic.

She pulls a thermos from the basket, finds two paper cups and gets ready to pour drinks.

HAZELMAE

The grass is dirty.

NORA

Then so is the sky.

HAZELMAE

I don't know why we didn't go with the rest of the girls in the first place.

NORA

Because they're children. God, they're so young!

HAZELMAE

It couldn't be because Mistah Pipe-Smoker is in charge of the picnic?

NORA

I am bored with Mistah Pipe smoker's love affair with himself. And his hair is too long.

HAZELMAE

You weren't bored until he laughed at your Valentine.

NORA

I knew—I knew that I shouldn't have told you about that.

HAZELMAE

You didn't. I was there.

NORA

Then why make me feel like a fool all over again?

Nora hands Hazelmae one of the paper cups.

Happiness.

HAZELMAE

What's in it?

Toasts.

Happiness.

She drinks.

NORA

Gin and pineapple juice.

HAZELMAE

Not very much gin.

Notes to the director/teacher and the actors:

Now we cut back and forth between Nora and Hazelmae; these are medium-close shots approximating the girls' distance from each other on their respective parts of the picnic blanket. When we get to Nora's line, "He's cute," Hazelmae should join Nora in the medium-close frame, suggesting that she has moved towards Nora to get a better look at The Boy. When both actors appear in the frame, then their bodies nearly fill the frame.

NORA

Then you steal it next time. Your father doesn't drink as much as mine, anyway.

Off in the woods we hear the sound of woodchopping.

My father! All fathers! The only time they appear is when we are in danger of enjoying ourselves.

Lying back and relaxing in the sun, Hazelmae says:

HAZELMAE

My papa calls me "honeybucket."

NORA

Is there one single, sane, logical reason why we couldn't have gone to that house party? I ask you!

HAZELMAE

I have blanked it from my mind.

NORA
(mimicking)

"Young ladies don't go to house parties with young gentlemen until they're eighteen." Why? Do they ever tell you why? "Because they don't dear."

Nora looks off into the woods where she has heard the chopping. She takes out her glasses, the better to see the woodchopper.

I loathe it when they call me dear.

(a beat)

He's cute.

Nora puts away her glasses. Hazelmae sees where Nora is staring.

HAZELMAE

Ohhhh—Yessssss.

NORA

I saw him first.

HAZELMAE

All we'll do anyway is talk about him. Simmer down, lamby-pie.

NORA

Simmer yourself down, pie-face. One summer in Nashville three years ago is no excuse for that accent.

Notes to the director/teacher and the actors:
I have Hazelmae react to Nora, and then move away from her, the camera panning with Hazelmae. She lies back down on her side of the blanket before she says, "If you can arbitrarily change your name to Nora, I can certainly change my accent."

HAZELMAE

If you can arbitrarily change your name to Nora, I can certainly change my accent.

Notes to the director/teacher and the actors:
From another camera position at least 45 degrees from the previous camera setting, we see both girls in the frame. This is

a medium shot that encompasses both the girls and most of the picnic's baggage, such as the cosmetics case, the picnic basket, and the thermos. After Hazelmae's line, ". . . I am definitely unemancipated," she looks up, startled. Nora's eyes follow hers. Then we cut to a low shot of The Boy, looming above them. This medium-close shot of The Boy from the girls' POV should suggest that The Boy has some of that "sexual swagger" discussed in the text and represents something both appealing and threatening to the girls.

NORA

If you just once looked into something besides a mirror—

HAZELMAE

Such as, pray?

NORA

Such as the works of Ibsen, pray—you'd know Nora was the first emancipated woman.

HAZELMAE

Lamb, the purpose of my accent is to make certain that before I am twenty, I am definitely unemancipated.

We see THE BOY looming above them. He looks down on them. He is about eighteen, wearing faded trousers and carrying a soiled T-shirt. He stands and looks at them for a long moment, finally focusing on Nora.

THE BOY

Hi-yuh.

Notes to the director/teacher and the actors:
   From this point forward, we cut back and forth between medium-close shots of the two girls and The Boy looming above them.

NORA

Hi.

HAZELMAE
(weak, scared)

Hi.

THE BOY
(after a moment)

You live hereabout?

NORA

Yes.

THE BOY

Not in the village.

NORA

No.

HAZELMAE

Huh!

THE BOY

I do.

NORA

Oh, but I like the village. It's charming. The atmosphere of these little old—

He suddenly bursts into laughter.

Well, I happen to think it is charming.

THE BOY

Huffy.

NORA

When I choose to be.

                           HAZELMAE
                            (to Nora)

I just wouldn't talk to him at all.

                           THE BOY

Nobody's talking to you, fatso.

                            NORA

That's mean.

                           THE BOY

I give back as good as I get.

He wipes his brow with his forearm.

                            NORA

    What's the matter? Hot?

                           THE BOY

    Damn.

Notes to the director/teacher and the actors:
    *From another camera position, we have a profile of Nora
and The Boy with Hazelmae sliding into the background, wary
of the exchange going on between her friend and this Boy. Nora
hands The Boy the thermos. He takes a short drink, makes a
face of surprise, and then takes another drink. He sinks slowly
to his knees in front of Nora. He stays close to her through the
line, "I'm pretty near through." Then he gets up, the camera
following him as he moves back into the woods. After a moment,
we then cut to a two-shot of the girls.*

She hands him the thermos. He takes a short drink, makes a face of
surprise, and then takes another.

                           THE BOY
                           (cont'd)

Well! What dya know now!

Again he laughs—but with a sexual joyousness this time.

What dya know! Got a smoke?

He takes the cigarette she offers. He sticks it behind his ear.

Gonna be here awhile?

NORA

Yes.

THE BOY

Got a murderous job but I'm pretty near through.

He goes back into the trees.

HAZELMAE
(forgetting her southern accent)

We're leaving.

Nora looks after The Boy.

NORA

We just got here.

HAZELMAE

Stop showing off.

NORA

I'm not doing a thing.

HAZELMAE

He's filthy and he smells.

We can hear the woodchopping in the background.

NORA

Hazelmae, you're a snob.

HAZELMAE

You're not even old enough to go to a house party.

NORA

What makes you old enough? House parties? What they say? No, it's everything that's bothering you inside and saying: Do!

HAZELMAE

You're not impressing me one bit. Now come on.

The woodchopping stops.

(frightened)

Nora . . . please come.

NORA

Nothing is going to happen. I can take care of myself.

HAZELMAE

If your father finds out—

NORA

Think I care?

HAZELMAE

Please! Let's hurry before—

Off-camera, we hear The Boy laugh. The girls look up, startled.

Notes to the director/teacher and the actors:
For the next seven lines, we move back and forth between medium-close shots of Nora, Hazelmae, and The Boy, as appropriate.

The Boy has returned to the clearing. He is stripped to the waist, his T-shirt dangling out of a rear pocket. He kicks the thermos so that it rolls to Hazelmae. Fearfully she picks it up. He grins.

THE BOY

Running to Momma?

NORA

No.

THE BOY

Kids scare easy.

He leans down to Nora, blowing into her ear.

Boo.

NORA

I'm not a kid.

THE BOY

Well?

NORA

Well?

Notes to the director/teacher and the actors:
From another angle, we see The Boy move over to Hazelmae.
He gives her the picnic basket. Nora is off camera.

The Boy takes the picnic basket and gives it to Hazelmae.

THE BOY

Wait up at the road.

HAZELMAE

She's coming with me.

NORA

We are together.

THE BOY
(to Hazelmae)

Wait up at the road, kid.

HAZELMAE

Nora—

THE BOY

The baby's afraid of the woods.

Notes to the director/teacher and the actors:
We cut to a medium shot of Nora, who is looking at The Boy and Hazelmae. After Nora tells Hazelmae that she'll "be along in a minute," we cut back to a medium two-shot of Hazelmae and The Boy. Hazelmae hesitates, but The Boy gestures with his head for her to go. After a moment, she turns and runs quickly from the clearing. The Boy watches her go, and then the camera pans with him as we walks over to Nora.

NORA

Don't hang on me, Hazelmae. I'll be along in a minute.

Hazelmae hesitates but The Boy gestures with his head for her to go. She looks at him, at Nora, and then runs quickly from the clearing. Nora smiles.

It's very pretty here, isn't it?

THE BOY

It's pretty.

NORA

In summer, everything is so tender. Except the colors. I mean—

THE BOY

The colors're soft in the shade—

He picks up the blanket. He walks to the edge of the clearing leading into the woods.

Notes to the director/teacher and the actors:
The camera pans with The Boy as he walks with the blanket to the edge of the clearing. At the edge of the clearing where the forest begins, he turns back to Nora. We cut back and forth between The Boy and Nora as each speaks. These are whole body shots. When he says, "Then come on," The Boy extends his hand towards Nora. The second time he says, "Come on," we see the action from a profile angle as Nora walks into the frame. She walks towards him slowly, then reaches out and takes his hand. He leads her into a darker part of the forest.

THE BOY

You been here before?

NORA

Yes, but—

THE BOY

You're not just all big talk?

NORA

No.

THE BOY

Then come on.

NORA

I . . . I should really . . .

The Boy has walked towards a clump of trees in a darker part of the woods. He turns, extends a hand out to her.

THE BOY

Come on.

After a moment, she walks slowly towards him, then reaches out and takes his hand. He leads her into a darker part of the woods.

FADE OUT

THE LOVESONG OF
ALEX VANDENBERG
Episode 1
by
T.J. Walsh

Just out of college and new to Hollywood, T.J. Walsh is a young writer who has already rewritten two screenplays for low-budget producers. He took these rewriting assignments with the proviso that he would not be given screen credit. A graduate in journalism from San Diego State University and with an MFA in Drama from the University of Texas at Austin, Walsh has had plays produced on both coasts. He has worked as a copy boy, drama critic, and sportswriter on various newspapers. Although two of his original screenplays have been optioned, Walsh is still awaiting that joyful day when he can see his name listed in the credits as screenwriter.

ALEX VANDENBERG, fresh from a divorce, leaves California for Texas to teach English at the University of Texas at Austin. Unprepared for the culture shock that follows a sudden change from Berkeley, California, to Austin, Texas, Alex meets DOROTHY TRAVIS, a very attractive, thirtyish teaching colleague who aspires to the position of dean of the English Department. Dorothy and Alex seem to be natural antagonists, and this is the state of their relationship during this scene. This delights TYLER BENNETT, a graduate student, who can barely disguise his amorous feelings for Dorothy. Tyler, gawky and unsure of himself in personal relationships, takes joy in needling Alex. Later, Alex and Dorothy will become lovers and even now, in spite of their differences, there is a kind of unconscious sexual attraction to each other. For all of his blend of precocity and social ineptitude, Tyler is eminently likeable and eventually he and Alex become good friends.

INT. HALLWAY, ENGLISH DEPARTMENT. DAY.

DOROTHY is walking down the hallway, turns a corner, and is greeted by a very long line of students waiting outside her office, the office that she reluctantly shares with ALEX. She smiles at the students and enters.

Notes to the director/teacher and the actors:

The screenwriter's description of the action that establishes the scene is good. It is a proper choice to have Dorothy walk down a hall that is not filled with students before she turns the corner and encounters the long line of students outside the office she shares with Alex. These visual images set up the premise of the scene before the action begins.

INT. DOROTHY AND ALEX'S OFFICE. DAY.

ALEX is sitting at his desk pulling a sandwich out of a brown paper bag. He opens a can of Diet Coke, looks up at the portrait of Shakespeare, raises the Diet Coke in salute, and drinks.

Notes to the director/teacher and the actors:

The first shot of Alex should be across his desk. He is burdened with piles of papers. Rifling through them, he finds the can of Diet Coke, opens it, and raises it in salute. We then cut to another camera position that should be over his shoulder and focused on a portrait of Shakespeare; Shakespeare should look as if he appreciates the toast.

We cut back to the across-the-desk shot that shows Alex drink from the can and then turn to see Dorothy as she comes in through the door. The camera pans with his look so that we see her. She smiles in his direction and the camera follows her over to her desk opposite Alex's and she sits down. The ensuing conversation cuts back and forth with medium shots of each teacher seated behind the desks.

DOROTHY enters, looks at him and is amused, and then moves to her desk and sits. He looks over at her, not too pleased.

ALEX

I want to thank you.

DOROTHY
(cool, distant)

You're welcome.

ALEX

It was quite a surprise this morning. When they sprang
it on me.

DOROTHY

Grace Peabody is ill. I had to appoint someone. It's my
job.

ALEX
(grumbles)

Yeah, yeah . . .

DOROTHY

Somebody's got to be the freshman advisor.

ALEX

Yeah, but why me? I'm new here. I don't even know the
system.

DOROTHY

That's all right; neither do they.

Notes to the director/teacher and the actors:
*Following her line, ". . . neither do they," we hear the door
open and Dorothy turns to look at who is entering. The camera
cuts to a medium shot of Tyler, who starts speaking to Dorothy
and then turns to his right as he notices Alex.*
*When he continues speaking, he is turned in Alex's offstage
(o.s.) direction. The camera cuts back and forth between the
two men through Alex's line, "I can feel it." If this scene is
edited, the first cut from Tyler to Alex should come after, "Hey,
Dorothy, I . . ." and then back to Tyler for his "Oh, hi" to
Alex.*

This does not need to be a special camera move but only needs to be a visual insert of Alex's action just before he mutters "God only knows..." in a medium close shot. Camera moves are saved this way, which saves both time and money.

TYLER enters.

TYLER

Hey, Dorothy, I . . .

He sees Alex. Tyler smiles. Turns to Alex.

Oh, hi. You've got quite a line of kids out there. Must be close to a hundred. What's holding you up?

ALEX
(mutters)

God only knows.

(with more vigor)

It's lunch time. Lunch. Five letter word. Certainly you've heard of it? Second meal of the day. Even someone as low as the freshman advisor gets a lunch break, doesn't he?

TYLER

The sooner you see them, the sooner they'll be gone.

ALEX

They'll never be gone. They're like amoebas. They're multiplying out there right now. I can feel it.

Notes to the director/teacher and the actors:
Starting with the moment when Tyler extends his hand and the two men shake hands, the action should be framed in a two-shot of Tyler and Alex from Dorothy's point of view (POV). Every so often during the conversation between the two men, we should cut to a reaction shot of Dorothy as she watches the psychological battle between the two men. She is amused.

These reaction shots of Dorothy should all be shot in sequence after the rest of the scene has been shot to eliminate un-necessary camera position moves. This gives the editor as many options as he may want in the cutting of the scene.

Tyler extends his hand. They shake.

> TYLER

Alex, isn't it?

> ALEX

That's right. It's short for Brenda.

Tyler smiles a smirk. Alex smirks back.

> TYLER

You're teaching the graduate seminar on the 20th Century Novel, right? 1920 to 1940.

> ALEX

That and three freshman comp courses.

> TYLER

I'm going to be taking your course. I'm finishing up my Master's thesis this year on Thomas Wolfe.

> ALEX

What are you keying on?

> TYLER

Autobiography. In his novels.

> ALEX
> (a little sarcastic)

You're really going to have to do some digging on that one.

Alex puts some books on a shelf.

> My dissertation was on Eliot's "The Love Song of J. Alfred Prufrock." Autobiography was my key, too.

TYLER

> I think I read that. "Autobiographical Elements from Eliot," right? It was published, wasn't it? Yeah, in the MLA or something, right? You were at Berkeley, weren't you?

ALEX
(rather pleased)

> Yes . . . yes, I was.

TYLER

> Yeah, that's right, yeah, Vandenberg. I remember it. I thought it was full of holes.

ALEX
(punctured)

> Really? Fortunately the doctoral committee didn't share your opinion.

TYLER

> No accounting for taste. They say it's about as tough to get a doctorate at Berkeley these days as it is to get a Social Security card.

Tyler smiles. Alex speaks with forced calm.

ALEX

> Ichabod, isn't it?

TYLER
(smug)

> No, Tyler. Tyler Bennett.

Alex draws an imaginary line down the middle of the office.

ALEX

Ichabod, see that line?

Tyler looks down where Alex has drawn the imaginary line.

TYLER

No.

Tyler smiles, smugly.

> *Notes to the director/teacher and the actors:*
> *The director may want not only to shoot all of this action in a two shot, taking time limitations into account, but may also want to shoot the scene again in medium shots of Tyler from Alex's POV and Alex from Tyler's POV. This gives the editor many options since speeches like "Look harder, Tyler..." may benefit from a medium close shot's perspective.*
> *The same principle may apply to Tyler's line, "If you don't want any literary points of view but your own, why are you teaching?"*

ALEX

Look harder, Tyler. It's an imaginary line. You must use your imagination. It's sort of like longitude and latitude lines. Do you see it there, now.

TYLER

Okay, I see it.

ALEX

Don't cross it unless you're willing to risk bodily harm.

TYLER

If you don't want any literary points of view but your own, why are you teaching?

ALEX

I plan to brainwash all my students into my point of view.

Alex has taken a small coffee maker out of a box and is looking for a plug.

Are there any outlets in this room?

Notes to the director/teacher and the actors:
We cut to a different camera position that favors Dorothy. It should be a wide enough shot so that Tyler can enter the frame without changing the frame's size.

DOROTHY

Yes. But they're all on my side of the line.

She gives him a smirk.

Did you want something, Ichabod. I mean, Tyler?

TYLER

What? Oh, yeah. They said at the Bursar's office that you have to okay my classes before I can pick up my scholarship check.

He smirks at Alex and hands a card to Dorothy. She signs it.

Thanks.

Notes to the director/teacher and the actors:
We cut back to a two-shot of Tyler and Alex from Dorothy's POV.

He turns to leave, stops, and turns back towards Alex. Tyler then carefully steps his foot over the imaginary line and leaves.

Notes to the director/teacher and the actors:
We cut back and forth between Dorothy and Alex.

ALEX

The little twit.

DOROTHY
(cool, distant)

He's nearly your age.

ALEX

We're on two evolutionary planes. He's hovering right around nerd-pithecus.

DOROTHY

His I.Q. is in the top one percent of the nation.

ALEX

All those tests are culturally biased toward nerds.

Alex leans back in his chair, tired.

I'm exhausted.

DOROTHY

So am I.

ALEX

You? What have you done? Advised three graduate students and spoken at an alumni luncheon. I've been here since eight in the goddamned morning advising those squirming dormies out there that they have to take freshman comp before they move on to Chaucer, or that Touch Dancing 206K does not count toward their English credit even if a man named William Faulkner does teach the course! Grace Peabody isn't sick, is she? I know she isn't. I know she's home watching *All My Children* and laughing at me!

Notes to the director/teacher and the actors:
  When Dorothy gathers her things to leave, the camera should pan with her as she moves to the door. We watch her from Alex's POV. After she exits, we cut back to a close-up of Alex for his reaction shot, looking in the direction of her departure. His expression says, "trapped."

Dorothy gathers her things and starts to leave.

  Where are you going?

                    DOROTHY

  I've got an afternoon tea with the Daughters of the Alamo.

She exits. Camera catches his reaction—trapped!

                              FADE OUT

THE LOVESONG OF ALEX VANDENBERG
Episode 2
by
T.J. Walsh

ALEX VANDENBERG is a young Californian who has come to the University of Texas at Austin to teach English. He has just begun his first semester of teaching and is beginning to settle into his slightly dilapidated apartment. In this scene he meets KELLY DIXON, a very attractive 25, in terrific shape, who speaks with a charming Texas twang. She wears blue jeans, boots, and a tee shirt. She's wearing those green rubber gloves to help her clean the stove. Actually, what we first see of her is the rear end of this young woman, as the rest of her is in the stove, cleaning. And what we see of her leads one to think that this is, indeed, an attractive young lady.

Notes to the director/teacher and the actors:
This scene requires a utilitarian one-bedroom apartment, a locale not hard to find near most college campuses. With luck it will have one of those kitchens that is an extension of the living room and is separated by a work bar over which those in the kitchen can talk with those in the lounge-dining area. If possible, it is best to establish this scene with an exterior shot of Alex struggling along a path or outside corridor leading to the apartment door.

Alex should be carrying more items in his arms than he can safely hold: a big bag of groceries, a six-pack of beer, and his briefcase. At the door he juggles the three items and finally sets some of them down before he fishes the keys out of his pocket. Once his keys are found and the door is opened, we see him enter his apartment.

All of this physical action is set up before any dialog ensues, since it should have a kind of comedic quality about it that helps to set the tone of the scene. From the kitchen area with the

*work bar in the foreground, we see Alex close the apartment
door and then move quickly to the counter to unload his armful
of groceries. We see him astonished at what he sees.*

*Instantly, we cut to Kelly from his point of view (POV), her
head in his kitchen oven. Then we reverse the shot to see
Alex.*

ALEX

Hello! Who are you?

The young woman, startled, pulls her head from the oven.

KELLY

Oh, hello. Hello.

ALEX

Hello. Who are you?

KELLY

Kelly. Kelly Dixon. I live across the hall.

ALEX

Are you trying to gas yourself to death in my stove? It
won't work. It's all electric.

She smiles, and what a smile!

Notes to the director/teacher and the actors:
*During this exchange of five lines of dialog, I suggest that
you shoot medium close shots of the two performers, cutting
back and forth from each other's POV on their lines. On
Kelly's line, "No, no. I was just cleaning it for you . . . she
hadn't had a chance," film Kelly getting up from the oven and
moving towards Alex to stand on the other side of the bar facing
him.*

*For the next four lines, I would shoot over-the-shoulder
shots of Alex and Kelly from Alex's "Oh . . . great. Terrific . . ."*

until Kelly says, "Crystal told me." At this point I would move the camera position so that it is as far away from the work bar as possible, and we see Alex move to some unpacked boxes in the living room. He kneels down on the floor to unpack.

We lose Kelly from the frame as Alex is sorting out household items from the packing boxes so that we hear her voice offscreen (o.s.) when she says, "I'm a writer," and after a moment repeats, "I was saying I was a writer." She comes into the frame and kneels down slightly behind him as he is unpacking, but we see most of her in the frame as she explains, "I write short stories. I've sold a few. And I'm working on a novel. And you?"

"Alex should turn on his knees to face her on his line, "No. I read. I'm a reader." The editor should cut in the middle of the turn from Alex in the foreground (fg), Kelly in the background (bg), to a two-character shot from another camera position with the two actors in profile as Kelly starts to say, "You don't write?"

KELLY

No, no. I was just cleaning it for you. Crystal asked if I'd do it for you. She hadn't had a chance.

ALEX

Oh . . . great. Terrific. Don't let me stop you. You get paid for this, of course.

KELLY

Something off my rent. I also work part time as a teller at University Savings.

Alex takes a six-pack of beer out of one of the bags of groceries and opens one. He offers one toward KELLY.

No, thanks. English instructor, right? Crystal told me.

ALEX

Yeah.

Alex tiredly moves to some unpacked boxes in the living room and begins sorting through them.

                    KELLY

    I'm also a writer.

                    ALEX

    What?

He's concentrating on unpacking, preoccupied.

                    KELLY

    I was saying I'm a writer.

She leaves the kitchen and comes down to a chair and sits, watching Alex.

    I write short stories. I've sold a few. And I'm working
    on a novel. And you?

                    ALEX

    What?

                    KELLY

    I was saying I'm a writer. And you?

                    ALEX

    I'm a teacher.

                    KELLY

    Do you write?

                    ALEX

    No. I read. I'm a reader.

                    KELLY

    You don't write?

Notes to the director/teacher and the actors:

Shooting the two actors in profile and the fact that they are both kneeling down on the floor adds to the informal, casual feeling, perhaps even providing the feeling of potential sexual possibilities, in addition to the comedic feeling in the sequence.

Alex should get up as he says, "Without us, where'd you be?" We see Kelly by herself on the floor on the line, "Not at all? You don't write at all?" Then the camera should show us Alex standing in the doorway to the bedroom from her kneeling POV as he responds, "Not even letters. I don't believe in writing. Distorts the mind. It leads to cirrhosis of the liver." Alex smiles and exits through the bedroom door.

We then should cut to the bedroom door where we see Alex move across the room to the bed, which is laden with more boxes that need unpacking. Shooting across the bed with Alex in the fg sorting clothes, we see Kelly behind him, standing in the doorway.

ALEX

Don't look so disappointed. Readers are just as important as writers. Without us, where'd you be?

KELLY

Not at all? You don't write at all?

Alex moves toward the bedroom where more boxes need sorting.

ALEX

Not even letters. I don't believe in writing. Distorts the mind. It leads to cirrhosis of the liver.

INT. BEDROOM. DAY.

ALEX is looking through several boxes of books. KELLY appears in the doorway.

KELLY

Who's your favorite writer?

ALEX

What? I don't have a favorite.

KELLY

Everybody has a favorite writer.

ALEX

I don't.

He continues to look through the books, hoping she'll leave him alone.

KELLY

Everybody has a favorite writer.

Alex pulls a copy of Comedy of Errors out of the box.

ALEX

William Shakespeare.

KELLY

Come on . . .

ALEX

He's my favorite writer.

KELLY

I meant contemporary.

ALEX

What is this? Who are you?

KELLY

Who's your favorite contemporary writer?

Notes to the director/teacher and the actors:
Alex turns away from the bed to look at Kelly just before the line, "Look . . . go away . . . go home." The camera is re-

positioned so that we see Alex in profile as he completes his turn from facing the bed. Cutting from one camera position to another on a character's turn can often add to the energy in the scene from the audience's point of view.

Then, as Alex finishes his line, "... go home," Kelly enters the right side of the frame so that both of them are seen in profile as the dialog continues. Although Alex turns back for a moment to pull the first book he can find out of the box (it turns out to be Huckleberry Finn), he carries on this conversation with Kelly in profile.

Alex can't quite believe this person.

ALEX

Look . . . go away . . . go home.

KELLY

It's a simple question.

ALEX

Harold Robbins.

KELLY

No, really.

Alex pulls a copy of Huckleberry Finn out of a box.

ALEX

Mark Twain. Is he contemporary enough for you?

KELLY

He's dead.

ALEX

I'm an English professor. Death is a prerequisite to being considered great.

KELLY

Mine is Updike. For short stories. John Fowles for novels.

ALEX

Why Updike?

KELLY

Where are you from?

ALEX

What?

He can't quite keep up with this whirlwind.

KELLY

Where are you from? It's a simple question.

ALEX

Berkeley.

KELLY

California?

ALEX

I think so.

KELLY

God, I've always wanted to go to California.

Notes to the director/teacher and the actors:
On Alex's line, "Berkeley," he turns to the bed, picks up a box full of books, and starts back to the living room. When Kelly, behind him, asks, "California?" he turns and looks at her for a beat before he turns and heads out the door towards the living room on his line, "I think so."

From another camera position, we see Kelly follow him through the doorway saying, "God, I've always wanted to go to California." Alex moves towards the bookshelf with his box of books, but Kelly continues to pursue him.

Alex moves past her, into the hallway.

INT. LIVING ROOM. DAY.

ALEX comes down the hallway carrying his box of books. KELLY follows him.

ALEX

How's the stove coming?

KELLY

I've got to wait for the foam to settle.

ALEX

Oh.

Alex begins to fill some bookshelves with the books. Kelly sits down on the couch and just watches him a bit. Alex is aware that she's watching him and tries to ignore her. Finally:

KELLY

How old are you?

ALEX

What?

KELLY

How old are you?

ALEX

Over thirty. How old are you?

KELLY

Twenty-five.

Another long silence. Alex shelving books, Kelly just kind of looking at him. Alex becomes aware of the silence and the observation.

Notes to the director/teacher and the actors:
One method of keeping the scene interesting and comedic in intent while avoiding a static quality is to keep putting obstacles in Alex's way as Kelly continues to pursue him with questions. I'd put a small step ladder next to the bookshelf that Alex has to climb to put the books away on the top shelf. After a moment, Kelly can start handing books up to Alex on the ladder. These physical actions keep the scene light in feeling and keep Kelly from seeming burdensome with her continual questions.

She'll find his former wife's photograph at the moment she asks, "Have you ever been?" After the whole scene is shot, the director should shoot a close-up shot of Kelly holding the picture that will be inserted by the editor just before "Have you ever been?"

ALEX

How's the foam coming along?

KELLY

Are you married?

ALEX

What?

KELLY

Are you married? You look like the marrying type to me.

ALEX

No, I'm not married.

Kelly sees the photograph of Sarah sticking out of a box. She pulls it out and looks at the photograph.

KELLY

Have you ever been?

Notes to the director/teacher and the actors:

In his frustration, Alex heads back to the work bar and opens the six-pack that he put down along with the groceries after he entered the apartment. Kelly has driven him to drink! He opens the can of beer as she, having moved beside him, continues her questions.

We see all this action with the camera positioned in such a way that it can follow Alex as he goes around the bar to refer to the stove on the line, "That foam must be eating through the metal by now, don't you think?"

ALEX

For Christ sake . . .

KELLY

Well?

ALEX

Yes.

KELLY

How long?

ALEX

(mutters) A couple of years.

KELLY

How long?

ALEX

Seven years . . . almost.

> **KELLY**

This her? She's pretty.

Alex sees the photo of Sarah that Kelly has and grabs it from her. He stuffs it under a box.

How long've you been divorced?

> **ALEX**

Listen, Perry Mason—

> **KELLY**

I'm just curious.

> **ALEX**

Six months. Are you married?

> **KELLY**

Nope. Don't want to be.

> **ALEX**

Well, me neither. That foam must be eating through the metal by now, don't you think?

> **KELLY**

It takes awhile. Twain, huh?

> **ALEX**

Excuse me?

> **KELLY**

Twain? Mark Twain? So he's your favorite writer?

> **ALEX**

God, your mind jumps around. Yes, Mark Twain is my favorite writer. Of the ones I've read. But I haven't read you, of course. Yet.

Kelly jumps up and moves to the door, excitedly.

KELLY

Would you like to read some? I can go get some right now. It'll just take a second! You wait right here! I'll be right back! Don't move!

ALEX

Wait . . . but . . . I didn't . . . wait . . .

But it's too late. She's gone out the door.

Notes to the director/teacher and the actors:
Where the screenwriter describes the action as "But it's too late. She's gone out the door," the camera must show that action. That, however, should not be the end of the scene. First, we should cut to a medium-close shot of Alex's reaction to this whirlwind of a young woman, as he does what comedy directors would call a "take" that suggests his amazement. Then he should take a long, needed drink from his beer. This gives the scene a comedic finish that the audience can build on in their imaginations.

FADE OUT

THE LOVESONG OF ALEX VANDENBERG
Episode 3
by
T.J. Walsh

PAUL is a young Englishman who has been spending the past year teaching English in the United States. He has just concluded his second semester teaching at a large California community college. During this time he has been living in a typical California garden apartment. Living in the same apartment complex is KELLY, a young graduate student and hopeful writer. She has fallen in love with Paul, and the two have been having an affair.

EXT. STREET, OUTSIDE PAUL'S APARTMENT. DAY OR NIGHT.

Notes to the director/teacher and the actors:

Any campus building that can simulate the front of an apartment house can be used for shooting this scene. The entry way should approximate the appearance of an apartment house and should have a walkway that leads directly to the street. Ideally, this walkway should be about 20 feet long and lead to the street where Paul's car is parked at the curb. If the automobile can be a convertible with the top down, it will help in shooting the sequence and in suggesting the ambience of California.

The first shot begins as a long shot, which establishes the entrance to the apartment, and shows a couple of students walking towards the entry hall and going into the building. Then, we see Paul leaving the entry hall carrying a suitcase and, about eight feet behind him, we see Kelly over his shoulder as she dashes out of the apartment entrance and rushes to catch up with him.

Both actors walk directly towards the camera, which should be placed 18 to 25 feet from the apartment entrance. When

Paul is about eight feet from the camera, Kelly catches up with him, stops him with her arm, and they start to talk.

The long shot, then, has become a medium two-shot of the two actors. This means that the camera operator has refocused the lens as the actors have moved from the long shot to the medium two-shot.

PAUL

Setting his suitcase down and turning to Kelly.

Oh, hello.

KELLY
(a beat)

Don't you mean goodbye?

PAUL
(after a moment)

I'm . . . I'm going, Kelly.

Picking up the suitcase, Paul starts towards the camera moving from his point of view (POV) past the right side of the camera lens. In the background (bg), we see Kelly react and then hurry after him.

CUT TO:

**EXT. SIDEWALK, OUTSIDE PAUL'S APARTMENT.
DAY OR NIGHT.**

From another angle, we see PAUL come into the frame carrying his suitcase. A second later, KELLY comes into the frame; she catches up with him, stops him, and he puts down his suitcase again. They face each other.

Notes to the director/teacher and the actors:
This camera position is 90 degrees from the previous camera position. Since Paul walks out of the frame by moving past the right side of the camera lens in the previous shot, this second

camera position should be at a right angle to the first camera position. This camera placement helps the audience to understand where the characters have come from and know where Paul is heading. Consequently, when Kelly stops Paul, we then see the two actors in profile as opposed to seeing them from the front, as we did in the first sequence.

KELLY

Can't we see each other?

PAUL

No.

Paul once again picks up the suitcase, turns to the right, and moves out of the frame. Kelly reacts for a beat and then, once again, follows him out of the frame.

CUT TO:

EXT. SIDEWALK, OUTSIDE PAUL'S APARTMENT. DAY OR NIGHT.

PAUL walks to the curb, steps off, and walks around the car to the driver's door. Opening the door, he puts his suitcase inside and climbs in. Slamming the door, he is just about to start the engine when KELLY appears in the frame and, standing near the door, she talks to Paul inside the car.

Notes the the director/teacher and the actors:
The camera should be placed on the street side of the automobile so that we see Paul approach the camera from the sidewalk, go around the back of the car, open the door, and climb in. A second later, just as he is about to start the engine, Kelly enters the frame having followed him around the car offstage (os). As she enters the frame, she positions herself near the windshield so that she faces Paul in the driver's seat. All of this has been taken from one camera position with the camera operator refocusing as the characters move.

KELLY

You want to go, don't you?

PAUL

No. Your writing is—

KELLY

I could write with you around. I just haven't wanted to, that's all. My getting published is an easy out for you, isn't it? An easy way out of the relationship?

PAUL

Kelly, I—

Notes to the director/teacher and the actors:
  At this point, I would have most of the rest of the scene played in close-ups (cu's) of the two actors, cutting back and forth between them. For Kelly's cu's, the camera can come off its pedestal and be hand held from Paul's POV. Paul's cu's should be shot from Kelly's POV.

KELLY
(bitter)

You can tell youself you did the noble thing by leaving. You allowed me to continue with my art by breaking it off! That's just plain bullshit, Paul.

(softer)

You're afraid of commitment, that's all. You were dumped on by your ace-reporter ex-wife, and it's scarred you.

PAUL

That's not true!

KELLY

Then don't go!

PAUL

I can't do that to you.

KELLY

You mean you can't do that to you!

(silence)

I've gotten my share of rejection slips, you'd think I'd be used to this.

PAUL

I'm not rejecting you.

KELLY

You're not? Then answer me one question. When you leave. When you drive off aren't you going to feel relief?

(pause)

Honestly?

(pause)

In Parliament, Paul, silence is a vote of affirmation.

FADE OUT

Notes to the director/teacher and the actors:
After Kelly's line, ". . . aren't you going to feel relief," there should be a sufficient pause so that the editor can cut in Paul's reaction. Then the editor can cut back to Kelly for "Honestly?" After this, we cut back to Paul again as he must silently evaluate what Kelly has said. When we can see that he is unable to answer Kelly, in her next cu she says, "In Parliament, Paul, silence is a vote of affirmation."
After that, we cut back to a two-shot of Kelly and Paul. We can then see that he is turning the ignition key. We cut to a long

shot from a new camera position facing the automobile and approximately 15 feet distant from the hood of the car. Kelly steps back and the car pulls away from the curb. After the car has passed to the left of the camera, we stay focused on Kelly. The camera closes in on her until her face fills the frame as she watches the departing car. Finally, the frame should go to black.

MORNING GLORIES
by
Jeffrey Bloom

Jeffrey Bloom has written nearly two dozen features and television movies and directed seven of them. He believes that his best work is still ahead of him.

BARRY and DIANE are strolling by a pond at Heather Farms, a park that emulates natural streams, meadows, and countryside. He is a Welshman who has emigrated to the United States; he is about thirty. Diane, an American, is around forty. She is pretty, outwardly self-possessed.

EXT. WALKWAY AROUND POND. EARLY EVENING.

BARRY and DIANE are walking beside the pond. They stop, kiss, part, and then sit on a bench facing the pond. Diane pulls out a bag of bread crumbs and starts feeding the ducks.

Notes to the director/teacher and the actors:
This is a very simple, straightforward scene to be shot outdoors somewhere on campus. If the campus has a pond, then part of the action should be shot with that body of water either in the foreground or the background of the establishing shot. If the campus does not have a pond, then, perhaps, the scene should be shot in a woodsy part of the campus. Where the screenwriter suggests that Barry and Diane should be walking beside the pond, I think the scene can be more effective if it opens with a long shot of the couple, preferably from the other side of the pond, with them in the distance.
We should be able to tell in the frame that they "stop, kiss, part, and then sit on a bench facing the pond." Shooting this first sequence in a long shot helps convey a greater romantic feeling. A return to the same long shot at the end of the

sequence, with the lovers parted, will give the scene greater resonance. Once the characters are seated on the bench, then the camera should cut to a medium shot of both characters, as Diane pulls out a bag of bread crumbs and starts feeding the ducks.

Just before Barry starts to speak, we should cut to our third shot, a medium-close shot of all of Barry and part of Diane, sitting close together on the bench.

BARRY

I lived with my grandparents . . . I never told you that, did I? Truth is . . . I hardly knew my mother and father. Anyway . . . my grandfather was a blacksmith, one of the few left in Wales. They used to say that the forge he built was the loveliest in all of Wales. My grandmother was an artist. Her hands were like wands and whatever she touched became something beautiful. And she played the harp. Oh, what an ancient instrument it was, too. We traced it back, once, all the way to the late sixteen hundreds, would you believe? She would only play it about once a month, but always on holidays, and particularly on Christmas. The whole family would gather around her . . . my two brothers, our sister . . . and she would play, and sometimes we would sing, for as long as three hours of an evening.

(a pause)

Up in those valleys, there wasn't any television, you know. We had to do something, didn't we?

A silence. Then, with a little grin.

Notes to the director/teacher and the actors:
The camera should change positions before Barry begins a new "beat" with the line, "I'm avoiding the issue, eh?" Probably the best shot would be over Diane's shoulder facing towards him as he turns to face her more directly on the bench. After he

asks his question, then we should cut to an over-the-shoulder shot from his POV of Diane as she responds.

Then we should cut back and forth on their speeches to over-the-shoulder (slightly different positions than usual since they are sitting beside one another on the bench). This way of shooting the scene can continue through Barry's line, "And your punishment." Then the camera should get a close-up of Diane on her speech and go back to Barry on his speech that begins, "You know what you've got to face..." and ends with, "Or stay where you are and feel nothing at all."

I would also shoot Diane's reactions to what Barry is saying; they can be incorporated by the editor as appropriate during Barry's long speech.

                          BARRY
                         (cont'd)

I'm avoiding the issue, eh?

                          DIANE
                         (nods)

Yes.

                          BARRY

Well, why not? You know what they say: "life is too foolish to take seriously."

                      (Pause. Then)

They do say that, don't they? Well, someone must, I'm certain of it.

A pause. Then,

                          DIANE

It has nothing to do with what happened this morning, you know.

                          BARRY

I didn't think it did.

DIANE

What those women think doesn't matter.

BARRY

That's how it should be.

DIANE

But I do care about you.

BARRY

I know that.

DIANE

And I'm too old for you!

BARRY

That doesn't matter!

DIANE

It could never be anything but temporary, Barry. You've always known that.

BARRY

I've never believed it.

DIANE

I'm a married woman.

BARRY

You make it sound like a fatal disease.

DIANE

I don't mean to. Only a permanent condition.

BARRY

Which is okay . . . as long as it's not a coward's condition.

DIANE

Maybe it is. But then it's my excuse, isn't it?

BARRY

And your punishment.

DIANE

Well, it's mine either way, and I'll just have to live with it. With that, and with my husband, and our two children, and our home, and our dogs and cats and respective in-laws, and our social and moral obligations, and all the rest that comes with fourteen years   of   marriage.

A pause. Then,

BARRY

You know what you've got to face, Diane? You have one man who can give you everything but love, and another man who can give you little else but love. So which do you choose, eh? Either way you have something to win and something to lose. But if you're lucky, life is a long-term proposition. Pain gets eased away by happiness pretty quick. But the kind of misery you have from living a life that's only half what it could be starts to nibble away at your insides, and after a while you don't care much any more because you don't really feel much any more. And that's what you're up against now, my love. You can fly away with me, and bear the pain. Or stay where you are, and feel nothing at all.

Notes to the director/teacher and the actors:
   After the screenwriter writes, "Silence again," the camera should cut to a full two-shot of their bodies. We see Barry reach

out to take Diane's hand. She allows him to hold it for a moment, but then she drops his hand and stands. At the moment that she starts to turn away from him in the two-shot, we should cut back to the camera position across the pond, the same long shot that opened the scene. From this shot we should see Diane complete her turn away from Barry and walk away until she is out of the frame. Barry sits on the bench, desolate and alone. The scene fades out.

By cutting back to the same long shot that opened the scene, we are doing what some directors call "framing the scene" and adding to its resonance.

Silence again. Only the birds singing in the distant trees. Diane's eyes fill with tears. She stands. Barry reaches out to take her hand, and she allows him to hold it for a moment, but then she lets him go and walks away.

FADE OUT

WATSON, SHERLOCK, AND ME
by
T.J. Walsh and Leslie Abbott

J. S. HOLMES, son of a wealthy San Francisco merchant, was born in London although he has lived all of his life in the San Francisco Bay area. A successful young scientist, Holmes, who is only thirty, has been able to live out his fantasies—and his major fantasy has been to emulate, indeed become, the twentieth century Sherlock Holmes. He has discovered a "DR. WATSON" working at the UC San Francisco medical center. Promising him the monies with which to open a private practice, Holmes has enlisted Watson's help in solving his first "case." As the action begins they are in a dance studio of the San Francisco Ballet Company watching PATRICIA JAMES, a slightly over-the-hill dancer with the company.

INT. BALLET STUDIO. DAY.

We see HOLMES and WATSON quietly enter one of the ballet studio rehearsal rooms. Against one of the walls is a row of mirrors and a barre.

Dancing by herself is PATRICIA JAMES. She is dancing the suicide sequence from the ballet *ROMEO AND JULIET*, that leads up to the moment when Juliet takes the poisoned potion.

Just as she is about to arrive at that climactic moment she spots in the mirror the images of Holmes and Watson. She stops abruptly, surprised that she has been watched.

Notes to the director/teacher and the actors:
This is a rather nice shot if you have access to a dance studio on campus. Patricia turns away from the mirror and faces Holmes and Watson. As she addresses them, we see their responses in the mirror behind her. This is a slightly tricky shot

*since we must not see the camera and crew in the mirror as well.
It can be done with a little juggling of the camera position.*

HOLMES

The suicide sequence from ROMEO AND JULIET.

PATRICIA

Yes. Who are you?

HOLMES

You dance it very well.

PATRICIA

It was planned that I was to dance the role this year.

WATSON

I'm Doctor Gregory Watson and —

HOLMES

And I am . . .

He and Watson exchange looks. Watson's look says: "don't say
'Sherlock.'"

I am J. S. Holmes.

Notes to the director/teacher and the actors:
   *We cut to another camera position so that the action is seen
in profile without any studio mirrors in the background.
Patricia moves towards the two men so that all three appear in
the frame.*

PATRICIA

That's right. I knew I had seen you before. Jason's son,
right?

HOLMES

Yes.

WATSON

You dance all the leads for the company, don't you?

Notes to the director/teacher and the actors:
The camera pans with her as she walks over to a bench, sits, and starts massaging her leg. After the camera has panned with her, Holmes and Watson can no longer be seen in the frame. Then after Patricia says, "Things have changed," we cut back and forth from the sitting Patricia to the standing Holmes and Watson.

PATRICIA
(wiping her face with a towel)

Did. Things have changed.

HOLMES

Alexandra?

PATRICIA

Among other things.

WATSON

You were suppose to dance Juliet?

PATRICIA

Yes. I'd kill for that role. Romulus finally scheduled the thing for this season and then —

WATSON

Alexandra.

PATRICIA

That little Russian has always had bad timing.

WATSON

Until now.

Patricia laughs.

PATRICIA

Why all the questions?

HOLMES

You've heard about the murder this morning, haven't you?

PATRICIA

Yes. Robbery, wasn't it?

HOLMES

The police aren't sure.

PATRICIA

I didn't know her very well.

HOLMES

You lived in the Soviet Union for awhile, didn't you?

PATRICIA

My father worked in the Embassy in Moscow. For six years.

HOLMES

So you speak the language?

PATRICIA

I did. Fluently. But not any more. No one to practice with.

Notes to the director/teacher and the actors:
From another camera position at least 45 degrees from the previous camera positions, we see Patricia seated on the bench while Holmes moves over to her with Watson following. As Holmes sits down beside her on the bench, he pulls a piece of

*paper from his pocket. Before he starts to speak, we cut to a
two-shot of Patricia and Holmes on the bench; although Watson
is nearby, he does not appear in the frame.*

Holmes takes out a piece of paper from his pocket. He hands it to
Patricia.

HOLMES

Can you, by any chance, tell me what this means in
Russian?

Patricia looks at it. Her face shows nothing.

PATRICIA

Mectb? Why it means . . . well, revenge, I guess would
be the most comprehensive translation. Why?

HOLMES

Just curious.

She hands the paper back to Holmes. Standing up, Patricia moves over
to the studio's exit doors. At the door she turns back.

Notes to the director/teacher and the actors:
    *As Patricia rises, the camera tilts up and pans with her to the
exit door. When she turns back to face Holmes for her final
line, she should be in a medium shot that shows her from head
to toe.*

PATRICIA

You know, Mr. Holmes, that killed the cat.

HOLMES

Yes, Ms James, I'm well aware of that.

Notes to the director/teacher and the actors:
    *The camera cuts back to Holmes for his final line. He rises
before he speaks, and as he does, Watson enters the frame to
join Holmes in watching the departing ballet dancer.*

FADE OUT

SIMON AND CAROLE
by
T.J. Walsh and Leslie Abbott

Simon and Carole is a comedy suspense thriller. CAROLE is the editor of an alternative investigative weekly newspaper published in the San Francisco Bay area. In addition, she teaches a couple of journalism courses at the University of California, Berkeley. She is an attractive, bright, clever, gutsy newspaper woman. SIMON is a financially comfortable man in his thirties whose brother is the publisher of the alternative newspaper. Carole doesn't know it but Simon is also the celebrated "S.J. Burton," a top-flight political reporter for the New York Times; he is staying incognito in Berkeley at his brother's home during a sabbatical from the Times while he writes the "Great American Novel." Simon is definitely attracted to the feisty, good looking Carole.

Notes to the director/teacher and the actors:

Although I co-wrote this screenplay and originally set the action in a university parking lot, I believe there are more interesting campus locales available for the scene. Whenever possible, I try to have vertical levels on which the actors can perform, since this invariably leads to more interesting visual shots.

In recent filmings of this scene, I've shown Carole and Simon in a medium-long shot descending the outside stairs of a modern school building. Halfway down the steps, they are stopped by Carter's calling out to them from the top of the stairs; it is obvious that he has been trying to catch up to them.

I then cut to a medium shot of Carole and Simon, who, stopping on the stairs, say their first two lines of dialog. Right after Carole says, "It's Berkeley," Carter shoves into the frame, squeezing tightly between the stair rail and Carole. Now the medium shot is filled by all three actors. It has a crowded look to it that I think adds to the comedic effect of the sequence.

EXT. FACULTY PARKING LOT, UNIVERSITY OF CALIFORNIA. DAY.

SIMON and CAROLE are walking back from the classroom to the car. After a moment, CARTER REED, the lanky student, runs to catch them. Carter is Carole's nemesis, largest supporter, class enthusiast, and class antagonist. He is the brightest and the best. For Carter, being good necessitates also being a rebel. His ongoing conflict with Carole is that the print media is dead, long live the broadcast medium. He's gotten McLuhan's message. Perhaps, deep in his heart, he still believes there's room for the printed word; but watching Carole's discomfort at his spoken beliefs is far too much fun. Under their adversarial roles, Carter has a not very well hidden crush on Carole; she is a little aware of it, pleased, amused.

He calls out to CAROLE.

CARTER

Carole, Carole. Wait a second.

Carole and Simon stop.

SIMON

Carole? The students call you by your first name?

CAROLE
(shrugging, explaining)

It's Berkeley.

(a beat)

Hello, Carter. I didn't see you in class.

CARTER

I was late. What's this I hear from Helen that you're using S.J. Burton's book?

CAROLE

Yes, I'm using it.

CARTER

Why, for God's sake? When you've got Dan Rather's book all—

CAROLE

Carter . . .

(pause)

Carter. This is print journalism.

CARTER

Broadcast journalism is investigative.

CAROLE

No, Carter.

CARTER

But—

CAROLE

Carter—

CARTER

The print journalist is dead. The most important part of a newspaper nowadays is its society page—

CAROLE

No, Carter. It's final.

Notes to the director/teacher and the actors:

After Carole has told Carter, "It's final," she and Simon descend the stairs, leaving the momentarily quieted Carter in a second or two of dejection before his usual ebullience leads him to press on. From another angle, we see him leap over the three remaining steps of the stairway, and look to the right and the left to determine which way the pair has gone. Spying them, he rushes in their direction.

From another camera position, we see Carole and Simon walking down a campus sidewalk. Behind them, running to catch up, is Carter. He practically pounces on them as he stops the couple with his next line.

CARTER

Who are you?

SIMON

No one you'd like, I'm sure. I'm a writer.

CARTER
(to Carole)

A friend of yours?

CAROLE

Simon Burton, Carter Reed.

The two men shake hands. Simon is trying to be friendly.

SIMON

Pleasure.

CARTER

You Carole's uncle or something?

SIMON
(weak smile)

Or something.

CAROLE

Simon's family owns the Bay Voice. He's a novelist.
He's here to work on one.

Notes to the director/teacher and the actors:

As Carter says, "Oh, Carole," I have Carole and Simon turn back to look at the departing Carter. As soon as they do, I cut to a medium shot, their POV of Carter, for the rest of the line, "We're having lunch tomorrow. The Yellow House. Right?" Then we hear Carole's voice offstage (o.s.) saying, "I can't Carter. I've got to go out to the foundation tomorrow. Some other time."

After this Carter says, again from the POV of Carole and Simon, "Then we'll make it dinner this weekend. See ya later." He should be trotting away by "See ya later."

Then, because it requires a smaller camera move, I put the camera in front of the path that Simon and Carole are taking and shoot them turning back towards the camera with Simon saying, "Cute kid," just before he and Carole pass by the side of the camera. Following this final shot of the scene, I have the camera moved to where Carter had said, "Oh, Carole," and from his POV, I shoot a medium shot of Carole and Simon starting with their turning to look at Carter through Carole's response.

When this shot is completed out of sequence, the scene is finished. In this way the camera has been used and the action employed in a way that lends a comedic feel to the material.

CARTER
(Drily)

Terrific. Well, I gotta go.

Carter starts to run back towards the stairs, stops, and calls out.

Oh, Carole! We're having a lunch tomorrow. The
Yellow House. Right?

CAROLE

I can't, Carter. I've got to go out to the Foundation tomorrow. Some other time.

Carter turns to leave.

CARTER

Then we'll make it dinner this weekend. See ya later.

He is gone.

SIMON

Cute kid.

FADE OUT

*Talia Crowell and Bob Vespa in **A MATTER OF CONSCIENCE**;
the Director of Photography is John Allred*

These seven shots from **A MATTER OF CONSCIENCE** show a traditional approach to shooting a film sequence.

(A) The first shot, an established shot, reveals both actors in a medium shot. Emotionally it suggests that the actress is relating to the incident in a different manner than the actor and that he perhaps questions her choice of action.

(B) As the actor turns to the actress, putting his hands on her waist, the camera refocuses from a medium to a medium-close shot. This camera lens zoom and his physical turning to her are done simultaneously so that the viewing audience is probably not even aware that the camera lens has adjusted to a tighter shot of the two characters. Generally speaking, camera moves that call attention to themselves are not good story telling. If the camera refocuses on a character's physical action it simply punches up the dynamics of the scene without the audiences' being aware of the mechanics involved in shooting the scene.

(C) At the appropriate moment in the scene we cut to the over-the-shoulder shot of the actor from the point of view (POV) of the actress. This cut reveals to us that the male character is concerned with the actions that the female character is taking.

(D) We cut to an over-the-shoulder shot of the actress from the point of view (POV) of the actor. She is explaining her actions to the man.

(E) We cut to a reaction shot, an over-the-shoulder shot of the actor from the POV of the actress; his reaction should indicate to us that he is troubled by her actions.

(F) We cut to a close-up (cu) of the female character as she trys to explain her actions.

(G) We cut to a close-up (cu) of the actor responding with some surprise and concern to her actions.

(A)

(B)

(C)

(D)

(E)

(F)

(G)

A MATTER OF CONSCIENCE

Episode 1

by

Leslie Abbott

FRANK and CULLEY are detectives with the Metropolitan Police Force. Frank is a university graduate whose swift climb in police work is the envy of Culley, a self-made man with a high school education. Both men are excellent detectives and usually get along well. The two men are on a college campus where a rally has just ended. The rally was organized to urge young people to fight an unpopular government policy regarding apartheid in South Africa. During the rally, Culley has impetuously pulled a microphone away from a black activist who was speaking at the rally. The student crowd became incensed by his action and it is only after the intercession of Culley's partner, Frank, that the crowd has calmed down.

> *Notes to the director/teacher and the actors:*
>
> *Many college campuses have outdoor steps that lead from one level to another. If you can find such steps, they are a good means of starting the action in this scene. Once the actors have started running down the steps, they should quickly start running past a school building. If that building happens to be brick, so much the better, since the configuration of brick as a background seems to evoke emotional responses in large proportions of audiences.*
>
> *As the two actors race alongside the brick building, they almost reach the camera's stationary position. Then Culley should reach Frank, grab him, and slam him against the brick wall. The camera pans with the two actors as this action transpires, and the cameraman should refocus during the pan so that the lens moves from a long shot to a medium-close shot all in one take.*

EXT. CAMPUS, STEPS AND WALKWAY. DAY.

FRANK, furious, runs down a series of steps and moves quickly along the walkway. CULLEY chases after him and finally catches up to him; he slams Frank against a wall.

CULLEY

Why don't you grow up, Sonny?

Pointing back towards the area where the rally took place.

> Guys like that are going to bring this country down . . . so that one of these days you'll wish to hell you didn't even live here.

> (pause)

We've gotta put them where they belong.

FRANK

Put who?

CULLEY

Radicals!

FRANK

And just who in the hell do you think are radicals?!

CULLEY

Guys like Rayford . . . standing on top of trucks . . . and trying to create riots!

FRANK

He's a kid! . . . There wasn't any riot going on . . . until you went there and damn well almost started one! You caused that fracas! They would have been upset, sure. But why add fuel to the fire?

CULLEY
(disgusted)

All I know is I do my job.

FRANK

What's that?

CULLEY

Protecting innocent people.

FRANK

And who's innocent in this case? I don't know.

(pause)

It looks to me as though you've made this decision already. The case hasn't come to court and you're handing out sentences already!

CULLEY

Somebody has to make the decisions.

FRANK

It isn't you, buddy . . . and the sooner you learn that the better.

Notes to the director/teacher and the actors:
As soon as Frank has said ". . . and the sooner you learn that the better," he walks to the right out of the frame. Culley reacts to Frank's statement, and then hurries after him.
We cut to another camera position where we see Frank heading directly towards the camera with the brick wall about eighteen inches to his right. After a few steps he stops; he doesn't know what to do about his partner's actions. Culley moves up and stops behind Frank's right shoulder and starts to

speak. Frank does not turn around to face Culley; he quietly listens, his eyes looking just to the left of the camera lens.

CULLEY
(quietly, meanly)

It's the spade chic . . . that's who it is . . . It's the spade chic, isn't it?

FRANK

Huh?

CULLEY

Don't bull crap me that you're trying to protect some kind of idealistic dream of this nation . . . You're protecting one person because you've got the hots for his sister! You're blinding yourself to the truth! . . . Kid?! My God, I was a kid one time, too, but I knew the difference between right and wrong!

FRANK
(forcefully)

Is black wrong and white right? Is that how you judge it?

Notes to the director/teacher and the actors:

Just before Frank says, "Is black wrong and white right?" Frank turns back and pushes Culley against the brick wall so that both men are standing in profile in relationship to the camera. After Frank's question that ends with, "Is that how you judge it?" Culley shrugs Frank off and moves right.

As he goes around the corner of the building and heads down a pathway, the camera cuts to a different position so that we see Culley, his back to us, striding away from the camera in a long shot.

A moment later we see Frank hurrying after Culley. About 30 feet from the camera lens, Frank catches up with Culley, grabs him, and turns him so that he is in profile on camera. As soon as they are squared off facing each other, we cut to over-the-shoulder shots of both men, as each speaks his dialog.

CULLEY

I was trying to stop him from putting foolish ideas into kids' heads that don't even know—

FRANK

And what ideas were you putting into their heads barging up there as a "big, white cop" . . . One man can put down a whole rally? What kind of ideas do you think you're putting in their heads, huh? . . . What do you think they're going to think of white cops from now on?

CULLEY

Yeah! Well, what are you going to do when your kids go to school? Huh? Trying to get an education . . . to learn right from wrong and respect for the law? And some white man or some colored man stands up there on top of a truck and says, "we're going to do this or that" . . . and your kid comes home to you with very little respect . . . and tells you, "I'm leaving school tomorrow, Dad, because nobody knows how to run this country . . . so we're going to take it into our hands."

FRANK

That's just what you're trying to do!

(pause)

That's what you were doing! Taking it into your own hands!

CULLEY

Somebody has to!

FRANK

You think you're the one to do it?

CULLEY

Yeah! I guess I may be the one to do it! Somebody's got to
do it!

Culley strides off across the quad. The camera moves in for a close-up
on Frank.

FADE OUT

Notes to the director/teacher and the actors:
   *We cut back to a two-shot of the characters facing each other
in profile. Right after "Somebody's got to do it!" Culley strides
away down the pathway. Frank follows him for a couple of
steps, then turns back facing the camera, his eyes slightly left of
the lens, as the camera zooms in for a close-up and a fade.*

A MATTER OF CONSCIENCE
Episode 2
by
Leslie Abbott

In this script a man, CHUCK, is discovered murdered in a shower of a Malibu resort motel in southern California. The homicide detectives learn that the murdered man attended a psychological "encounter" session that took place over a long weekend at the resort hotel. They learn that the encounter session was led by a well-known Beverly Hills psychiatrist, Dr. CARL (if the role is played by a man; CARLA, if the role is played by a woman) REINHEIMER. The detectives interview Dr. Reinheimer at his/her home and learn in the following flashback sequence what occurred at that encounter session.

Notes to the director/teacher and the actors:

In many respects, this is the most difficult scene among the screenplays in this book to direct or play. The scene is difficult to play for the actors because they must build the background of their characters with little other than this dialog to guide them. Furthermore, many of the characters are seen at a moment of desperation, fatigue, frustration, and anger; almost all of them have lost the character armor that usually protects them.

For the director, this is a difficult scene since it must be shot in such a way that the audience is always aware of the presence of all of the characters, even though some of them may be off camera for several minutes. In addition, the director needs to change the camera position constantly, which means that much time is used up moving the camera from one part of the room to another. This also means that the lighting must constantly be rearranged.

The shooting of the scene in snippets makes it doubly diffi-cult for the actors since they must never lose sight of their "through line of action," nor must they lose sight of how their characters' involvement in the scene builds and evolves. An attempt should be made to suggest an almost claustrophobic atmosphere in which the characters have a deep desire to escape from each other and are unable to do so.

Several campus settings may represent this meeting room in a Malibu motel: the green room of the theatre, a meeting room in the counseling building of the university, or possibly a meeting room in the college's student center. The seating should be in a kind of square, so that the participants can all easily see one another. Some of them are seated on sofas; others in single chairs. If there is any kind of table in the center of the seating configuration, it should be a very low table, which an actor could easily sit on during the action. If there is no low table, then a few lighter chairs that can be moved around in the action should be available so that one character can directly face another. (An example of this is when Barry sits beside Joyce and tries to confide to her that he, too, has attempted suicide.)

Since it is impossible to know what kind of room you will be using for this shoot, the camera directions can only be cursory suggestions.

INT. MOTEL MEETING ROOM—NIGHT

The encounter session is in progress. The motel meeting room is disheveled since the marathon session has lasted many hours and the maids and waiters have been cautioned not to interrupt the meeting. Styrofoam coffee cups are stacked up, ashtrays are laden with cigarettes. The camera follows CHUCK as he wearily walks over to a coffee urn, pours himself a cup of coffee and then returns to the group sitting on sofas around a large coffee table. The camera pans around the group starting with DR. REINHEIMER, an amiable nimble-witted person somewhere in his/her late middle years. As the camera pans we see CAROLYN, a wealthy, sophisticated woman, who is married to a nationally known sports promoter who owns the Los Angeles major league basketball team. Seated next to Carolyn is BARRY, a famous film director who is directing his first movie after several inactive years. To his left we see Chuck, a Las Vegas used car salesman. The camera continues to pan by the weary participants stopping for a moment at EFRAIN, an insecure young man who is concerned about his sexual identity. Finally, the camera stops at RAYFORD, a black militant who views the encounter session as a waste of his time; a judge gave him the option of either attending the session or spending a week in jail. Seated beside him is JOYCE, a timid young woman who has attempted suicide; she works as the social secretary for Carolyn. Rayford turns to Joyce.

> *Notes to the director/teacher and actors:*
> *Starting the action with Chuck at the coffee urn, eyeing the rest of the group, is essentially an establishing shot, which assists the audience in knowing who is in the scene and what their physical proximity is to one another.*

RAYFORD
(He pulls back the sleeve of JOYCE's to
reveal that her wrist is heavily bandaged)

Is this why you're here?

JOYCE

You shouldn't have done that . . .

Surprised and a little alarmed, the group realizes that she has tried to commit suicide.

> *Notes to the director/teacher and the actors:*
> *A long portion of this scene should be shot from three different camera positions so that the editor can cut back and forth between principal actors and the rest of the cast, who are reacting to the action at a given moment. Starting with Rayford's pulling back Joyce's sleeve to reveal her cut wrist, the scene should continue through Barry's line, "I don't think there is anything to pursue."*
> *The first camera position should focus on Rayford, Joyce, and, part of the time, Barry. The second camera position*

should focus on Chuck, Carolyn, and, part of the time, Barry. The third camera position should focus on Efrain and Carolyn. Once the dialog has begun, the only person who moves around through this sequence is Barry, which explains why he is only in each camera position part of the time.

There should be a fourth camera position picking up a portion of the scene, starting with Barry's line, "Never," and continuing through his speeches that conclude with, "I'm sorry." This fourth position should record Barry in both medium-close shots and close-ups, depending upon the moment in the action.

Each time the scene is repeated from these different camera positions, the actors must take care to replicate their physical actions and their emotional choices so that in the ultimate editing of the scene, each actor's work is consistent in the final cut.

RAYFORD

Did it hurt?

JOYCE

I know this sounds terrible . . . but . . . I was at peace for a while. Just everything drifted . . .

RAYFORD

Why don't you act like a woman instead of a little white rabbit? Where's your confidence, girl?

Barry, looking at Rayford, asks:

BARRY

Have you ever wanted to kill yourself?

RAYFORD

No.

Carolyn, who has been following the action silently, turns toward Chuck.

CAROLYN

Have you?

CHUCK
(savagely)

No! Why don't you try it!

The camera pans with Barry as he gets up from where he has been sitting and moves over to Joyce.

BARRY

What do you do?

JOYCE

No one wants to bother with me . . .

Barry sits beside Joyce

BARRY

Go ahead . . . tell us . . . we're all interested in each other.

Joyce looks around the group nervously.

JOYCE

Well . . . I don't see why anyone . . .

From Joyce's point of view (POV) the group is looking at her with concentrated interest.

JOYCE

I mean . . . why bother about me?

BARRY

Because you and I happen to have something in common.

JOYCE

Really?

RAYFORD

You tried to kill yourself?

BARRY

Yes.

RAYFORD

How?

BARRY

The usual way . . . sleeping pills.

EFRAIN

Did you . . . did you really think you'd go?

BARRY

Of course I thought I'd go . . . I hadn't made a picture in five years . . .

CHUCK

Who saved you?

BARRY

I think in the end I saved myself . . .

Turning to Joyce, Barry changes the subject.

What do you do?

JOYCE

I . . . I don't do much . . . some substitute teaching . . . I work part-time as a social secretary.

BARRY

Are you a good teacher?

Shaking her head.

JOYCE

No . . . I'm not.

BARRY

Is there something you're good at?

JOYCE

I used to . . . I used to write.

BARRY

Are you good at writing?

JOYCE

I don't know.

(Pause)

At times I wrote stories . . . and I thought they were different and unique.

BARRY

Anyone ever see them?

JOYCE

Yes. . . there was this man at the university I went to . . . he thought they were pretty good.

BARRY

And you didn't go on from there?

JOYCE

No.

BARRY

Why not?

JOYCE

Oh . . . I don't know . . . you want your life to be so
private, you know . . . and you feel so stupid . . . you send
those things out in the mail and you try to sell something
and it's just so stupid . . . I mean, don't you feel stupid
when you're directing?

Getting up quickly, Barry steps to the center of the room. The camera
pans with him, the group in the background (bg).

BARRY

Never!

JOYCE

You're so exposed!

BARRY

Never!

(after a beat)

That's what saved me . . . it was knowing after all those
years of being blacklisted . . . of being damned . . . having
doors shut in my face . . . Me! With an Academy Award!
They had convinced me that I was dead to this world . . .
and then I thought . . . between the booze and the
nembutals . . . I thought: "I'm good! I'm genuinely good
at what I do . . . and what a terrible waste . . . what a
terrible waste it would be if I were to die" . . . that
stopped me!

After a moment, Barry moves back to Joyce.

I think you have to find that you're a good writer and
continue to know that you're good . . . and I don't care
what you're good at . . . a good librarian . . . a housewife
. . . a "lay" even . . . but you're good!

Barry turns away, a bit embarrassed.

I'm sorry.

REINHEIMER

Don't be sorry, Barry. You say you don't let things get through to you.

Notes to the director/teacher and the actors:
Once the action of this sequence has been shot from the three separate camera positions, as well as the pick-up of Barry's action from a fourth camera position, then I think the director should do a pick-up of Reinheimer's speeches starting with "Don't be sorry, Barry," and continuing through the speeches until Reinheimer has said, "People don't always know when they want help. Finish what you started to say."

REINHEIMER
(cont'd)

Shouldn't you let all things get through to you?

BARRY
(vehemently)

No! You build eight foot walls made of steel to keep them out!

(pause, uncomfortable)

Besides . . . I don't have anything to prove.

CAROLYN

Wouldn't you be a better director if you let people get close to you?

BARRY

No.

EFRAIN

What about now?

BARRY

What about now?

EFRAIN

What are you now?

BARRY

Fortunately . . . I'm directing again . . . Except for this stupid weekend.

REINHEIMER
(to Barry)

Why do you think they wanted you to come here?

BARRY

I haven't the vaguest idea.

REINHEIMER

Well, there must be a reason.

BARRY

I don't know what it is.

CAROLYN

I think I do.

BARRY

You think you do?!

REINHEIMER

Why?

CAROLYN
(quietly)

You constantly call yourself a film director and not a man.

REINHEIMER

What?

Looking at Barry and speaking louder.

CAROLYN

You constantly call yourself a film director and not a man. And that's where your problem is . . .

BARRY
(angry)

I don't understand this Freudian crap!

CAROLYN

You can't help anybody who doesn't want any help.

REINHEIMER

People don't always know when they want help. Finish what you started to say . . .

Carolyn turns to Barry, facing him squarely.

CAROLYN

Don't you really know why you're here? Or are you just afraid to say?

BARRY

I do not know why I'm here.

CAROLYN

Do you act the same way on the set as you do in this room?

BARRY

That's none of your business!

He turns his back on Carolyn.

CAROLYN
(pressing)

Obviously it must be the reason with the people who
hired you . . . or they wouldn't have you here.

Turning to face her.

BARRY

What?

Carolyn speaks louder.

CAROLYN

Obviously it has something to do with the people who
hired you or they wouldn't have you here.

(pause)

You have to work with people.

Barry sits, not answering. The camera moves around observing the
group. They are silent.

EFRAIN

Carolyn . . . you were saying something to him . . . and
then you stopped . . . something went wrong . . . You
stopped pursuing something.

Barry interrupts.

BARRY

I don't think there is anything to pursue.

He walks away from Efrain and Carolyn going to the coffee urn where he
pours himself a cup of coffee. Barry can be seen in the bg getting himself
a cup of coffee.

Notes to the director/teacher and the actors:

There are a number of ways that the ensuing action in this scene can be done. I choose to have the action shown by a shot of Barry moving over to a free-standing table where he goes to get coffee. By putting the table away from the wall, it is possible to shoot Barry across the table so that he appears in the right foreground (fg), while we see Efrain, Joyce, and Carolyn past Barry, seated in the left side of the frame.

Barry stays facing the camera and reacts to their comments. Just after Efrain says, "How do you think he is," Barry turns to face Efrain, Joyce, and Carolyn. From this point forward, the camera cuts back and forth from Barry's POV to the three actors' POV.

When Barry turns, the next few shots of him should be from the POV of Efrain, Joyce, and Carolyn, showing him in the left side of the frame. Think about it for a moment and you will recognize the logic of Barry's placement. A moment later, Chuck steps into the right side of the frame, joining Barry, and he points towards Carolyn on his line.

The way these camera set-ups and cuts have been made will inform the audience that Barry is referring to Carolyn. From the point where Chuck joins Barry in the frame to declare, "It's just bitches like you rubbing him the wrong way," to Chuck's conclusion, "They're never happy unless they're hurting you," we simply cut back and forth between the two conflicting groups.

When the camera is seeing Barry and Chuck from Efrain, Joyce, and Carolyn's POV, the pedestal has been lowered to their seated eye level, and when Barry and Chuck are seeing the other three actors seated, it is shot with the pedestal at their eye level.

EFRAIN

He changed the subject.

CAROLYN

Because he's afraid of himself . . .

EFRAIN

You mean because he thinks he's better than everybody
else?

CAROLYN

Yes . . . that's part of it. But he wasn't that way with
Joyce.

JOYCE
(quietly)

I don't think he means to be that way . . .

EFRAIN
(reacting to Joyce)

How do you think he is . . .

Turning to the group from the coffee urn where he has been stirring sugar
into his coffee. He is annoyed.

BARRY

I wish you wouldn't talk about me as if I weren't here!

Chuck moves into the frame with Barry. He points at Carolyn as he
speaks.

CHUCK

It's just bitches like you rubbing him the wrong way.

EFRAIN

Why do you call her a bitch? To you every woman is a
bitch. What's the matter?

CHUCK

It's just the way it is!

BARRY

I agree with you . . .

RAYFORD

Oh, man! You do nothing but put each other down!
Sick! Sick!

CHUCK

Ah! . . . At last! A few words from the colored contingent!

RAYFORD

All you honkies really hate women, don't you?

BARRY
(ironically)

Isn't it always true . . . there's got to be something wrong
with you . . . if you disagree with a woman! You've got to
be a fag . . .

CAROLYN

Oh? And you two are so macho?

CHUCK

Very funny!

Barry turns to Chuck, reassuring him.

BARRY

Don't let it bother you . . . I've had it all my life.

CHUCK

They're all ball breakers!

BARRY

If you don't respond the way they want you to, there's
something wrong with you.

CHUCK

You're one hundred percent right! They live to break balls. Every one of them. That's their sole function. They're never happy unless they're hurting you.

Notes to the director/teacher and the actors:

During the next exchange of dialog between Efrain and Chuck, starting with Efrain's line, "What makes you hate women so," and conluding with, "And you judge all other women because of what she did to you," we cut back and forth with medium-close shots of the two men only.

After Efrain's line ". . . because of what she did to you," we return the previous focusing on Efrain, Joyce, and Carolyn in one shot and Barry and Chuck in the other. It is important to note that the focusing down on Efrain and Chuck does not require any alteration in the camera set-ups. It is simply a matter of focusing on the individual men during their exchange of dialog.

Anytime that you can avoid a change of camera position through careful preplanning, you are saving the production company considerable expense. The script suggests during this sequence that, "In the bg we see some of the other members of the encounter session. They are watching Chuck intently." This insert should be shot following the conclusion of all the other camera set-ups in the scene, simply to save both time and money.

EFRAIN

What makes you hate women so?

CHUCK

They just use you . . . don't you understand?

EFRAIN

I'm not that sure yet . . .

CHUCK

You'll find out . . . Broads use you! Then they move on
to the next victim . . . they give you love and happiness . . .
so-called . . . you provide them with a home, a car, and
they're gone! Users! All of them.

EFRAIN

Did you love her?

CHUCK
(quietly)

Did I love who?

EFRAIN

The one that . . . went off.

In the bg we can see some of the other members of the encounter session.
They are watching Chuck intently. After a moment:

CHUCK

Yeah . . . I loved her . . . very much.

EFRAIN

And you judge all other women because of what she did
to you?

Notes to the director/teacher and the actors:
   *At this point, the camera pans with Chuck as he returns to
his seat. On the line, "You agree," Chuck looks up and Barry
sits down beside him saying, "Absolutely! You had one . . . "
From this point forward, we cut back and forth between Barry
and Chuck on one side and Efrain, Joyce, and Carolyn on the
other, until Barry has said, "I can recommend a good prostitute!"*
   *As we cut back to Carolyn with her question, "Male or
female," the camera should focus solely on Carolyn. Then it
cuts back to Barry and Chuck. This exchange of dialog should*

continue with this framing until Carolyn has said, "I sort of thought you'd want a young boy." We then cut to a wide-angle shot that reveals all of the people in the group.

Rayford gets up and moves away from the group. We then cut to a close-up of Rayford as he delivers the film's final line.

CHUCK

That's the way it is . . .

Turning to Barry for support.

You agree?

BARRY

Absolutely! You've had one . . . I've had five. Five women in a row! Over fifteen, twenty years . . . all the same.

EFRAIN

Did you leave them?

CAROLYN

They were smart . . . they left him!

CHUCK
(disgusted)

I can just see your son! The same situation.

CAROLYN

That's not true! My son doesn't have a problem!

CHUCK

I'll bet.

EFRAIN

I don't think I have a problem . . . It's just that . . . my mother . . . makes me think I do . . . She twists everything . . . and . . . I come to the conclusion . . . I'm wrong. But I know I'm not. It's just that—

BARRY

I suggest you try shouting back at her . . . just once . . . and see what happens.

CHUCK

Why don't you get yourself a girl who isn't nice . . . ball the hell out of her!

CAROLYN

That's just the kind of suggestion . . .

CHUCK
(emphatically)

Just ball the hell out of her!

EFRAIN

Does that come natural?

CHUCK

It has to come natural.

BARRY
(to Efrain)

I can recommend a good prostitute.

CAROLYN

Male or female?

BARRY
(ignoring Carolyn)

I've got a whole studio full of them . . . they stand in line as soon as they find out you're a director . . . the broads are crawling at you in Hollywood!

CHUCK

That's right.

CAROLYN

Is that what you want . . . a woman? I sort of thought you'd want a young boy.

RAYFORD

Oh, man! You're all fools! Sick, sick fools!

FADE OUT

A MATTER OF CONSCIENCE

Episode 3

by

Leslie Abbott

JOYCE, a young woman in her mid-twenties who lacks self-esteem and has had little sexual experience, works as a social secretary for CAROLYN. Carolyn is a glamorous woman in her forties who is married to JAY, a wealthy man who owns a major league basketball team and a huge sports arena in Los Angeles. LANCE, an attractive, masculine young man in his early twenties, is her son from a previous marriage. In this scene, Lance and Joyce have gone on a date that ends with the two of them parked on a hilltop of Mulholland Drive in Los Angeles. Unknown to anyone, Lance is having an affair with an older man. This particular script is a "shooting script" with the scene broken down into various shots by a film director.

EXT. HILLTOP, MULHOLLAND DRIVE—NIGHT

EXT. LONG SHOT—CARS, HILLTOP

It's late at night and a star-filled sky stretches out over the sparkling lights of Los Angeles. The camera pans along the cars parked along a "Lovers' Lane," stopping when it reaches LANCE'S car.

MED. SHOT, INT. CAR, NIGHT

The camera pans to the darkened car's back seat where we see the commingling bodies of JOYCE and LANCE. They are petting heavily. He is kissing her passionately and she is responding in kind. Carefully he takes her coat off and removes his own as the two continue to pet.

JOYCE
(whispering)

Do you love me?

LANCE

Yes.

JOYCE

Do you really . . .

Lance does not reply but starts to unbutton her blouse. Joyce begins to unbutton his shirt. The two kiss again.

MED. CLOSE SHOT—JOYCE

Point of view (POV) of Lance.

JOYCE
Please . . . I need to know . . . Do you love me?

MED. CLOSE SHOT—LANCE, JOYCE

He doesn't answer, instead continues to kiss her.

JOYCE

. . . It isn't that you just want . . .

Lance puts his hand across her mouth stopping her questions. He doesn't want to talk. He doesn't want to profess love for her. After a moment he brings her legs up under him and starts pressing against her body. He continues for a moment and then abruptly stops kissing her and sits up. He starts to take his shirt off so that it is hanging loosely around him; he is not wearing a tee-shirt. Clumsily, he tries to unbutton her blouse. Fumbling, he can't get the blouse open.

LANCE

Take your blouse off!

Joyce begins to take her blouse off. It slips from her shoulders and we see her in her slip.

JOYCE

Do you love me? Tell me . . . Do you love me?

Unable to answer her, Lance starts to kiss her passionately. After a moment she asks:

> Not just physically . . . I mean: . . Do you really love me?

Lance pulls away from her. He is angry.

LANCE

> What the hell is the matter with you!?

Joyce pulls him toward her.

JOYCE

> No . . . I mean it. "I love you."

He struggles to say the words.

LANCE

> I . . . love . . . you.

She caresses his hair, feeling his face tenderly.

JOYCE

> Look at me and say it . . .

LANCE

> I want to make love to you . . .

JOYCE

> No . . . No. Say it! "I love you." Say it so I know you mean it . . . say "I love you."

MED. CLOSE SHOT—LANCE, JOYCE

From another angle. He starts to kiss her tenderly, moving his kisses to her neck, brushing her hair, moving his hand down toward her breast.

She holds him tenderly, her body quickening as she begins to feel passion for him. Suddenly Lance begins to sob. He cries for a few moments.

                    LANCE

Oh . . . God!

                    JOYCE
                  (alarmed)

What's wrong?

CLOSE-UP—LANCE

He is crying softly.

                    LANCE

I . . . I can't . . . it won't happen . . .

MED. CLOSE SHOT—JOYCE, LANCE

Joyce is puzzled; she doesn't know what is wrong. Lance pulls himself away from her reclining body. He touches her tenderly but we can see that he is not able to make love to her. He whispers.

                    LANCE

I'm sorry . . . I'm sorry, Joyce. I wanted to . . . I just wanted to go to bed with you . . . I don't love you . . . I just wanted to have sex with you . . . but I can't do it . . . Do you understand me? I mean . . . nothing happens.

CLOSE-UP—JOYCE

Joyce's eyes close. She is crushed, blaming herself for the failure to excite Lance.

MED. CLOSE SHOT—JOYCE, LANCE

After a moment Lance looks at her; he is quietly angry now.

                              LANCE

   It's all your fault, anyway.

Pulling away from her, he starts to button his shirt.

      Get dressed!

Putting her hands over her face, Joyce is devastated. Beginning to cry, she shrinks into the corner of the back seat. Lance grabs her and pulls her upward handing her the blouse.

      Get dressed!

She falls back into the corner of the seat, quietly sobbing.

      It's all your fault, anyway. All your silly talk!

MED. CLOSE SHOT—LANCE

He is buttoning his shirt and straightening his clothes. Now JOYCE'S crying becomes more audible. Angry and frightened, he turns to her as he struggles with his clothes.

      Stop crying! Get dressed!

After a moment he finds her coat and shoves it toward her.

      Here! Put your coat on!

Joyce is crying loudly now. Lance doesn't know what to do. He is angry and hurt, frightened that he can't get aroused.

      Stop crying! If you're gonna keep that up . . . you can just
      get out and walk home!

MED. CLOSE SHOT—JOYCE, LANCE

From another angle. Joyce is unable to answer him. Slowly she turns looking at him and seeing him in a different light.

      It's your fault . . . all your silly talking! That drivel about
      love . . . You don't have to love somebody to . . .

He stops talking, filled with the realization that it's easy for him to make love when he does love the person. Joyce's crying continues. For a moment he is tender, wanting to help.

Come on . . .

CLOSE TWO-SHOT—JOYCE, LANCE

From another angle.
Lance reaches over to help her. Joyce pulls away from him.

JOYCE

Don't touch me!

LANCE
(angry)

Well . . . then get out!

Joyce doesn't move. She is crying softly. After a moment, Lance leans towards her.

Joyce . . . I'm sorry.

(a beat)

Look! You won't say anything, will you? You won't tell . . . you won't tell Jay, will you? Or my mother?

Joyce doesn't answer, her face registering no reaction. After a moment.

LANCE

Joyce? . . .

She nods her head from side to side.

Joyce! Tell me you won't!

She continues to nod her head from side to side.

Say it!

> (pause)

And after we get back it will be just like nothing ever happened. All right?

Joyce is silent.

Talk to me! Like nothing ever happened. All right?

Joyce begins to whisper over and over.

JOYCE

. . . Like nothing ever happened. Like nothing ever happened . . .

Lance looks at her with concern.

LANCE

Like nothing ever happened!

Quietly, over and over, Joyce repeats:

JOYCE

. . . like nothing ever happened . . . like nothing happened . . . nothing happened.

When she continues to murmur "nothing happened," Lance finds her words grinding into him.

CLOSE-UP—LANCE

LANCE

All right . . . all right!

CLOSE-UP—JOYCE

JOYCE

Nothing happened!

CLOSE-UP—LANCE

> LANCE
> (frightened, angry)

SHUT UP!

CLOSE-UP—JOYCE

After a moment.

> JOYCE

Nothing happened . . .

> (a beat)

Nothing happened.

CLOSE-UP—LANCE

He looks at her with a blend of pain and anguish lacerating him.

> LANCE

It was your fault it didn't happen.

CLOSE-UP—JOYCE

> JOYCE
> (barely audible)

Nothing happened . . .

                                        DISSOLVE

TWICE DAMNED, ONCE BLESSED

by

Leslie Abbott

MICHAEL and TERRY are young residents of a private hospital for the mentally disturbed. Both boys are in their mid-teens. Michael was brought to the hospital by his parents after he tried to commit suicide. He has been diagnosed as a schizophrenic. Terry asked his parents to commit him to the hospital because he has wild mood swings that terrify him; he has been diagnosed as a manic-depressive. Terry's parents do not believe he should be in the hospital and are convinced that he can be well if "he'll just stand on his own two feet."

Notes to the director/teacher and the actors:

This scene could just as easily be played by young women in a private hospital for the mentally disturbed. It can be filmed in one of the larger dressing rooms, washrooms, or shower rooms of the campus theatre department.

In this scene, the director can explore various possibilities, including filming Michael and Terry's images in the mirror and then, as one of them turns away from the mirror, have the camera pan away from their mirrored images to their actual faces. Sometimes you can have one actor's image in the mirror while the other actor is actually facing the camera.

As in other scenes in this book, I suggest the director explore those times when the camera should have a two-shot, an over-the-shoulder shot, or a close-up. I have purposely not been more specific about how the shots should be framed and where the cuts should be made in this scene, since that will be dictated, in part, by the locale in which the scene is filmed.

INT. HOSPITAL. LAVATORY OF THE WARD. NIGHT.

The camera sees the men from behind catching their faces reflected in the metal mirrors above the basins. They are all in a row brushing their teeth before bedtime. The camera pans down the row; we see all the faces in the mirror: brushing, spitting, squinting, investigating blemishes, simply staring, mugging. The light is cold and hard—no illusion here. The camera stops on MICHAEL and TERRY, seen side by side in the mirror. Terry wears a robe and pajamas while Michael is in pants, stripped above the waist. They brush almost in unison, spit, wash out their brushes under the taps. Each turns slightly and addresses each other at the same time. Both boys are troubled. At the same time.

MICHAEL

Terry?

TERRY

Michael?

MICHAEL

Go on.

TERRY

No, you go on.

MICHAEL

Out there . . . during the fight . . . I couldn't hear anything. I thought I was getting well, but . . . Does anybody ever get out of here in a decent time?

TERRY

Some do. Ed Parrish did. Karl Sommers did.

(pause)

Williams, the fly-swatter, has been here thirteen years.

MICHAEL

What about . . . Tyler Haid?

Terry does not answer; he looks grief stricken.

What's the matter?

Terry looks straight ahead into his mirror, but starts to sway into the mirror; he lurches forward and uses the basin to support himself. Michael holds him around the waist and helps to hold him up.

TERRY

My parents . . . I got a letter. They want me home by the end of summer! God! That's only a few weeks away!

(near hysteria)

Isn't that too much!

MICHAEL

Oh, Terry . . .

TERRY

They think I've been playing games with them.

(quoting)

"There's nothing wrong with you that concentration can't cure . . . Two years behind in school . . . you'll never get into a good university. Your father wants you with us, and I quite agree. I'll send you a plane ticket and travelers' checks . . . You can stop on the way to buy new clothes . . . as long as we know where you are."

(strained, choked laughter)

As long as we know where you are!

He strikes his mirrored image with his fist. Michael grabs Terry and pulls him by the shoulders away from the mirror. Holding onto Terry's shoulders.

MICHAEL

Take it easy . . . easy.

We see the two boys in profile with their profiles reflected in the mirrors behind them.

TERRY

Mike . . . if we're going to have our day at the beach together . . . it better be soon. Please, Mike. Please!

Michael turns away troubled; it's difficult for Michael to commit himself to anyone.

MICHAEL

Yeah . . . okay . . . I promise.

Terry looks at Michael with affection. Terry puts his head against the mirror as Michael pats Terry's arm gently.

I promise.

The camera, from Michael's POV looks at the row of men. They are gabbing, horsing around. Mouths moving in loud talk. One snaps another with a towel—the other jumps and yelps. But, for Michael, there is no sound. We see Michael, still patting Terry, but he is frozen with fear caught in the dilemma of having a friend.

FADE OUT

CHAPTER 10

IT'S A WRAP!

On the final day of a film's shoot, when the actors, production staff, and crew wind up their contribution to the movie, and now it is in the hands of the post production people and God, the final moment of shooting is followed by the term, "It's a wrap!" This group of people has become a sort of family, and in some ways it is painful to say "good-bye," unless you're starting on the project of your lifetime next week. At such times, you recognize how much film is a collaborative method in which openness between writers, directors, producers, and actors is the greatest gift you can have.

During the shoot, when an actor speaks to the writer or director, more often than not, it is the actor's character who is talking. A good screen-writer or a good director knows that the actor's character is talking and that the actor wants to take their creations beyond the confines of the writer's script and the director's concept to the heart of who and what the character is about. That's what good acting is about.

The writer, the director, and the actors all look back on the concluded project and think to themselves, "Gosh! I wish that I had done that! If I had only had enough time, I'd have included this brilliant line of dialog, that piece of action that would have illuminated the text, that piece of business or inflection of voice that would have illuminated the moment." Well, film almost never allows you to perfect an idea or revise the movie on the basis of afterthoughts. Fortunately, writing about the art of filmmaking does. And "It's A Wrap!" provides me with the moment to add some afterthoughts:

LIFE AS AN ACTOR

Get your Bachelor of Arts degree, Master of Arts, or whatever in most professions, and this assures you that you will work for the rest of your life. Doctor, Lawyer, Merchant Chief, you can pretty much be assured that you will have, at worst, a good economic future regardless of how good you are at your work. You don't have to be particularly good, you don't have to hunt for your next job, and you don't have to maintain the personal discipline that you had during the first developing years of your career. The acting profession, conversely, constantly tests you all your life; you must continually work at your peak performance just to maintain a career.

The wag who said "you are only as good as your last picture" spoke wisdom. You must be a combination of artist and businessman, and this balance is essential to having a successful acting career. Add to that, an element over which you have no control, luck. You must have the luck to get the right role at the right moment in order to have that career blossom. There are few professions where one can have outstanding skills, be hardworking and personable, and still not be able to achieve your objectives; acting is such a profession.

Maureen Stapleton has had an impressive and enduring career as a "star" on Broadway and as a fine character actress on both the large and small screens. She has enlivened the big screen with many memorable performances in such movies as *Cocoon* and *Stardust Memories.* She speaks from personal experience of the hardships that most actors must endure whether they succeed or not.

She says: "I believe in the toughness of actors. I have a feeling of genuine pride in actors as my people.... We're often called egomaniacs, irresponsible, stupid, unaware, and a kind of joke. We're accused of having big egos. Well, the actor's ego is no different in size because he's an actor. A writer or a painter or a musician can go off into a corner and lick his wounds, but an actor stands out in front of the crowd and takes it.

". . . Actors spend years and years being treated like dirt. They're constantly in a state of debasement, making the rounds of casting directors and having to look happy and great. I made the rounds for years, but I wasn't good at it. But then nobody is. You need a strong stomach. You need a sense of the business as a whole, so that you don't get lacerated every time somebody tells you you're lousy. You need strength and no matter how strong you get, you always need to get stronger."

Knowing when to head for Hollywood to pursue a film-TV career is important. For varied reasons, you must not delay initiating a film career until you are completely sure that your talent is honed to perfection and you can be certain that you can handle any acting challenges afforded you. If you were to do that, you would have probably squandered your youth. Producers, directors, casting directors, and audiences will excuse some of your inadequacies, be forgiving of your ingenuous qualities, and understand that as a young actor in films you can grow through experience and continued training.

If however, you wait too long to embark on a professional career, regardless of how good you are, there is a gnawing question going on in producers' minds: "Where have you been? Why haven't you got more film on you by now? What have you been doing with your life?" If you tell them that you have been working with a major regional theater somewhere out in America, it will mean little to them.

You may have been working at the Tyrone Guthrie in Minneapolis, the American Conservatory Theatre in San Francisco, or Long Wharf on the east coast, but to the average film person, working in such prestigious companies means no more to them than if you had been acting in a community theatre in Podunk. To start a career in Hollywood, you must have a legitimate resume of acting credits, but you must also be in Hollywood by a certain time and age or you're likely to miss the brass ring on the merry-go-round.

An actor must have the tenacity and courage to pursue a career after receiving defeats that would destroy the ego of most men. Nonetheless, from time to time an actor must realistically assess the state of his career, and sometimes that assessment may lead him to the conclusion that a successful career for him may no longer be possible. If after you've completed your acting training, you then spend five years pursuing a career, go to lots of interviews for jobs, have a diligent agent whose track record with other actors indicates that he or she knows the business and does well in it, and you have not seen much evidence that your career is on the ascendancy, then it may be time to consider moving into a different career. Knowing when to accept such a reality, regardless of how talented you may be, is one of the most difficult decisions an actor must make, but it can save you from a lifetime of heartbreak.

Most young actors, unfamiliar with the business, give up too quickly. A much smaller group stays long after a viable career seems unlikely. Knowing how long to stay and when to go may be the most important decisions you will ever have to make.

THE GENDER GAP

Actresses must look at the profession somewhat differently than men. When it comes to one's sex, Hollywood, like the rest of society, applies a double standard. The probability of an actress' enjoying a successful career is much less than that of an actor of comparable talent. In 1990, statistics released by the Screen Actors' Guild revealed that only 29% of the roles in screenplays and teleplays were written for women. Moreover, the same statistics revealed that actors earn twice as much as actresses.

While the middle years are financially golden for actors, an actress in the same category, regardless of her past "name" value and past track record, will see her opportunities vanish. At last count, women over forty were cast in less than 9% of all film and TV roles. Men may mellow with age, according to the myths maintained by middle-aged male producers, but women simply age. Even back in the 1930s, actress Bette Davis marveled that men "see themselves as permanently appealing and don't think it at all strange that they are making love to actresses who could be their granddaughters."

The irony, then, is that men can grow older without its threatening their careers; they dye their hair, wear corsets to suck in their paunch, and continue to work. Seeing aging actors with actresses twenty-five years their junior on their arms fuels the fantasies of the male members of the audience, and demographic studies reveal that the man has the final say on which movie will be seen when the family goes to the movie palace. The freezing out of women past a certain age, then, is primarily the result of marketing research, which the film financiers follow slavishly.

On the optimistic side, the demographics in the United States are changing rapidly, and this may alter the filmgoers' preferences in movies. For years, the 14 to 25 year-old age category has shaped the kind of motion pictures that have been made, but this age group is diminishing in size while the bulk of the population is rapidly aging. For the last twenty-five years, the person deciding which film to see was a guy under 25 who usually headed for action films.

In earlier times, when teenagers and the young male didn't dominate the movie-going public, there were women stars who often outdrew men at the box office: Barbara Stanwyck, Bette Davis, Joan Crawford, Carole Lombard, and Elizabeth Taylor come to mind. With the audience demographics changing rapidly, it's not possible to predict whether actresses will again receive a fairer share of casting opportunities. It can be plausibly argued that older audiences prefer stories involving relationships, feelings, and communication, and such films of necessity involve women.

There is already considerable evidence to support the notion that major box office draws in theatres are not always the shows that win the hearts of home video renters who watch their films at home on their VCRs; the home viewers are a somewhat older audience, and their interests seem to be somewhat different than the audience who goes to the movie theatres. These are somewhat hopeful signs that indicate women may play a more significant role in future casting.

AN ACTOR'S EDUCATION

George C. Scott, the eminently correct choice to play General Patton, once said in one of his more arrogant moments that he didn't believe in training to be an actor; he seemed to believe that actors received a God-given gift and either they could act or could not. It's the sort of non-sensical statement you might expect to find in a publicity story and perhaps, to be charitable, Scott was misquoted. Regardless, this comment certainly reinforced the thoughts of those lazy actors who have the notion that somehow you can have a career without a proper education.

There are certainly actors who have enjoyed successful acting careers without much education, but in recent years they have been the exception rather than the rule. Actors don't like to remember all those difficult years of training once they've achieved success, but an examination of nearly any actor's background in the last thirty years will reveal that most actors are well educated. The days when a film studio would guide an apprentice actor through a long training period that usually included developing both the actor's performing skills and their social skills as well is long gone. Now the actor must be a nearly polished product before he or she gets a chance to prove their worth on-screen.

Can talent be taught? Nobody can teach a person how to be imaginative or creative: that is a gift given to certain people who were lucky enough to have the right influences in their early years. The operative word here is "right," not "good." Many actors didn't have ideal childhoods, but something in their early formative years gave them imagination, creativity, drive, and the will to succeed. Those formative years cannot be minimized in how they contributed to eventual achievement in the performing arts. A drama coach/director/teacher tries to help foster such a person's talent so that it becomes whatever that potential permits. For the would-be artist, the hope is that you will find teachers and directors who have sympathy, empathy, and a capacity to enter into your mind without dominating it.

In universities and in acting workshops in New York, Los Angeles, and elsewhere, there are self-appointed gurus who, without intentionally doing so, have such a need to play Svengali that they try to make all their acting students into Trilbys. They have an enormous emotional need to be the person who shaped the persona of an actor—to receive their emotional strokes through the success of someone who hails them as the "influence" in the actor's life.

Sadly, it often leads to the kind of derision that was heaped on Lee Strasberg by such master teachers as Stella Adler, Robert Lewis, and Elia Kazan. Such a need on the part of the acting coach is folly; eventually, if the actor becomes successful, the actor will deeply resent such a teacher's need to receive full praise for the actor's work. Was that perhaps the reason George C. Scott was so disdainful towards acting training? Yes, of course, the acting coach/teacher/director is helpful as are any number of other people who cross the actor's life. There is something neurotic, though, in a teacher's need to dominate the life of an aspiring actor; there is also something neurotic in an actor who allows himself to become emotionally dependent on any authority figure.

Forfeiting your trust in your own judgment, becoming dependent on both the praise and criticism of others, does not augur well for an artistically rich and financially successful career. A good actor gets significant help from many sources, starting with parents and siblings, peers, kindly encouraging authority figures, and a host of teachers, many of whom know nothing about acting but have introduced the would-be performer to psychology, ethics, moral considerations, literature, sociology, and history.

Too many actors limit their education to theories of acting when they should be learning about human behavior, social institutions and their effect on mankind, religious thought and its virtues and faults in affecting mankind, political action and the weird need of some to wield power that so often betrays a man's best nature. In short, one way or another, fine actors learn about all kinds of cultures, all kinds of human behavior, every aspect of the human condition.

One of the reasons that it is so difficult to become a film-TV actor is that there are so many contradictory factors—all valid but seemingly at odds with each other—that apply to the profession that the actor must constantly sort out these differences and somehow make sense of them. For example, the absolute necessity that the actor must be capable of self-criticism and self-examination is always counterbalanced by the need for the actor to think well of and feel good about himself.

The actor must be able to recognize his skills as well as his limitations. It takes an enormously well-balanced, psychologically-sound person to be able to cope with all these conflicting messages that the actor receives. How can you be self-critical and think well of yourself simultaneously? Yet, both elements are necessary for the good actor.

AN ACTOR'S LIFE

And, finally, some words of wisdom from two people who have toiled mightily and well in films:

"The business would get to me. I didn't understand Hollywood. I didn't understand the mechanism behind the film industry. I had suspicions about what made it tick, about how people could be. I just had to have those suspicions confirmed, and they were. Then you're okay . . . It's cold. There's no room for emotional involvement. You can't be a monster—but you have to realize you're working in a factory, and you're part of the mechanism. If you break down, you'll be replaced, and there should never be any offense taken at people's attitudes. It's part of life there, it's the culture. Once you figure that out, it's easy."
—Mel Gibson, movie star

"What a strange business this acting is," Pyke said. "You are trying to convince people that you're someone else, that this is not me. You have to be yourself. To make yourself real you have to steal from your authentic self . . . the closer you play to yourself—the better. Paradox of paradoxes: to be someone else successfully you must be yourself."
—Hanif Kureishi in *Buddha of Suburbia,* screenwriter of *My Beautiful Launderette*

It's a wrap!

INDEX

Illustrations in **boldface** type

A

Abbott, Leslie: biography of, 297

Above-the-line personnel
listing of, 17–20

Acting Career
preparation for, xv
finding work in, xvi
reference works on, xvi
Michael Shurtleff, *Audition*, xvi
Tony Barr, *Acting on Camera*, xvi
Robert Cohen, *Acting Professionally*, xvi
M.K. Lewis, *Your Film-Acting Career*, xvi

Acting
and characterization, 69–75
and personalization, 75–78
preparation for, 67, 73–75
union membership, 80–81

Action
definition of, 3, 4, 5–6
film vs. stage, xiii

Actors
and competition, 28–29
and contracts, 106
and diligence, 110–112
and education, 287–289
and ego, 27–29
and energy, 33–35
and grooming, 82–83
and humor, 39–40
and instincts, 35–39
and life-affirmation, 40–41
and likeability, 102–104
and listening, 30–33
and rejection, 105
and role-playing, 41–45
and talent, 288

and thinking, 30–33
attributes of, 25–46
difference from actresses, 286–287
image of, 95–97
life as, 284–290
making contracts, 81–82
marketing of, 107–113
profile of, 79–80
pursuing careers as, 284–286
relationship with director, 49–55
visibility of, 108–110, 112–113

Actresses
and age, 286–287
and box-office appeal, 287
difference from actors, 286–287

Agents
getting one, 83–92
letters to, 84–86
nonfranchised, 89
using one, 92

Allen, Woody
and role-playing characters, 41
biography of, 158

Apocalypse Now
filming location for, **2**, **70**

Art director: definition of, 20

Assistant producer
See Associate producer

Associate producer: definition of, 18
seen from Assistant producer

Auditions
process of, 93–95, 100–101
Dustin Hoffman for *The Candidate*, 93–94
pieces, 94
as a performance, 97–99
cold readings, 99

ABOUT THE AUTHOR

LESLIE ABBOTT has worked with the National Broadcasting Company, Desilu Studios, Pasadena Playhouse, ZIV Television, Foothill College, and Diablo Valley College. He studied at the University of Pacific, New School of Social Research, University of Southern California, University of Shrivenham, University of London, and Stanford University. A former member of the famed Actors' Studio, the author has directed more than one hundred and fifty plays including the West Coast premieres of *Blues for Mister Charlie, All the King's Men, The Immoralist, Man with a Golden Arm, A Clearing in the Woods,* and seven original plays and musicals with his own company, Abbott-Abrams Productions. The author's previous textbook is *Active Acting.*